## Praise for *Until Every Child Is Home*

Fantastic! In an era plagued by unprecedented levels of family breakdown, Dr. Chipman's work could not be more timely or consequential. *Until Every Child Is Home* serves as a clarion call to the church by offering practical insights to a complex global dilemma. A wonderful reminder of Jesus' heart for the orphan and every Christian's responsibility to champion the cause of the fatherless.

**JAKE BARRETH**
Director of International Ministry, The Global Orphan Project

Every local church can play a part in successful orphan care. As a theologian, pastor, and parent, Todd Chipman shows the way in *Until Every Child Is Home* through the stories of couples who embraced adoption, churches that welcomed their new family members, and the key relationships parents should cultivate as they foster or adopt children.

**TAMMI LEDBETTER**
Managing Editor, Southern Baptist TEXAN

Todd Chipman doesn't just teach and preach orphan care; he's a product of orphan care, a passionate advocate for orphan care, and has led his family to be orphan-care exemplars. *Until Every Child Is Home* reveals Todd's heart, God's heart, and will help shape the heart of every reader on an issue that is, Scripture clearly states, the essence of true religion.

**PAUL CHITWOOD**
President of the International Mission Board (IMB) of the Southern Baptist Convention

*Until Every Child Is Home* is a theologically rich, practically helpful and personally engaging account of why the church must care for the most vulnerable. It will challenge you, encourage you, and inspire you no matter where you are on your journey!

**JASON JOHNSON**
National Director of Church Ministry Initiatives at CAFO

I'm so glad to see this book! Todd Chipman is a faithful and wise teacher who articulates the biblical foundations for orphan care and adoption, while also highlighting the practical challenges of engaging in this labor of love. I wholeheartedly recommend it for those considering adoption and/or those engaging in ministry to the orphan!

**TONY MERIDA**
Pastor for Preaching and Vision, Imago Dei Church, Raleigh, NC
Coauthor, *Orphanology*

It is amazing what God can do through your family and church if you embrace the biblical mandate to care for orphans. Not everyone is called to foster or adopt a child, but everyone can play a role in the care for children in need. In *Until Every Child Is Home*, Todd Chipman brings together what the Bible says along with the practical experiences of several couples that have adopted or served children through foster care. I highly recommend this book to parents who are preparing for their first steps in this journey or for churches that want to make orphan care more central to their faith family.

**KEVIN EZELL**
President, North American Mission Board, SBC

In *Until Every Child Is Home*, Todd gracefully makes the case for the church fulfilling James 1:27, to care for the widow and orphan in their distress. I'm deeply grateful for Todd's tender and truthful approach to child welfare. As someone who's been doubly adopted, by my heavenly Father and by earthly parents, I'm encouraged by this book on child welfare, and I commend it to be read and used by every church, as they seek to live out the gospel.

**CHELSEA PATTERSON SOBOLIK**
Author *Longing for Motherhood*
Policy Director, ERLC

# UNTIL

# EVERY

# CHILD

# IS

# HOME

## WHY THE CHURCH CAN
## AND MUST CARE FOR ORPHANS

### TODD R. CHIPMAN

MOODY PUBLISHERS

CHICAGO

Edited by Ginger Kolbaba
Interior design: Ragont Design
Cover design: Dean Renninger
Cover illustration of silhouette copyright © 2019 by Eladora / Shutterstock (179200187). All rights reserved.
Cover photo by Brian Babb on Unsplash.

ISBN: 978-0-8024-1906-4

We hope you enjoy this book from Moody Publishers. Our goal is to provide high-quality, thought-provoking books and products that connect truth to your real needs and challenges. For more information on other books and products written and produced from a biblical perspective, go to www.moodypublishers.com or write to:

Moody Publishers
820 N. LaSalle Boulevard
Chicago, IL 60610

1 3 5 7 9 10 8 6 4 2

*Printed in the United States of America*

*To my mother, Phyllis, and father, Roland (deceased),*
*who adopted me as an infant.*
*And to my wife, Julie, my partner for life.*

# Contents

# Foreword

In the days leading up to my writing this foreword, I found myself waist-deep in water, holding back tears. I was in the baptistery at my church, baptizing my son as my brother in Christ. He stood in front of me, taller than I am, a seventeen-year-old young man, but all I could see was the little baby he was when we first found him in a Russian orphanage. Specifically, I remembered being up all night praying for him after my wife and I learned that an antibody found in his bloodstream might mean he would be too sick to be released for adoption internationally.

My prayers coincided with reading the account in Genesis 43, in which Jacob's sons returned from Egypt to tell their father that the new governor had sent them back to retrieve their younger sibling, Benjamin, and return with him to Egypt. As I prayed that night, I could feel old Jacob's distress: "As for me, if I am bereaved of my children, I am bereaved" (Gen. 43:14). Even more than that, I took comfort in the promise of the brother Judah, who offered his own life as a pledge of Benjamin's safety. Judah would make sure, to his own hurt, that he would bring Benjamin home safely. And he did.

The baptism that day was a sign of that pledge, in the case of my own son Benjamin Jacob. Jesus, of the tribe of Judah, had offered up his life as a pledge of ultimate safety. The waters of baptism signified union with that Son of Judah in His life, death, burial, resurrection, and ascension. Baptism is, if we think about it, scary. One cannot breathe under water. It's meant to be that way—to be a signpost of the curse of the grave, of the waters of judgment, of the scandal of the cross. But baptism ends by picturing for us our own ultimate end—not descent into the abyss but a calling upward into newness of life. Baptism was a more important document of adoption than the paperwork we keep for Benjamin in a safe at the bank. In this case, the adoption joined him to the rest of us—all of us who have been adopted into the kingdom of God.

That's really what is at stake in the question of whether our churches will "care for orphans and widows in their distress" (James 1:27 NRSV): not whether we will extend some sort of *noblesse oblige* to the less fortunate, but whether we recognize who we are as the baptized people of God. We were orphans—homeless and destitute—who were given a place at the table of a loving Father, an inheritance of the entire cosmos, and a family bustling with brothers and sister from every tribe, tongue, nation, and language. Churches who learn to minister to orphans, to ex-orphans, and to their families, learn about more than just that ministry. They are learning what it means to be brothers and sisters, what it means to live on mission with Jesus, what it means to bear one another's burdens.

In *Until Every Child Is Home*, Todd Chipman, a wise and experienced guide on such matters, offers practical direction on how local congregations can do better in our quest to care for those Jesus calls "the least of these my brothers" (Matt. 25:40 ESV). This book will help you whether you are considering adoption or foster care, are thinking about how to minister to people who are in that process, or if you're simply skeptical about whether your church could ever have what it takes to enter this risky endeavor.

This book is no gauzy, sentimental "selling" of adoption or any other orphan ministry. Todd makes clear that this is spiritual warfare, and it brings with it a great deal of risk. But it's worth the risk. Water is risky too. An army of Egyptians drowned in it, and before that, an entire primeval population did too. And yet Jesus carries us through the water, at the start of our Christian lives, to show us that we have nothing left to fear and that, as was said of Him, we are beloved children in the sight of the Father. A church that is orphan-minded will be gospel-hearted too. This book will help show us how a ministry to fatherless children is about the nursery, yes, but it's even more about the baptistery.

RUSSELL MOORE
President, Ethics and Religious Liberty Commission of the Southern Baptist Convention; author of *Adopted for Life: The Priority of Adoption for Christian Families and Churches*

# Introduction

◆

# What You Need to Know About God's Goodness

Sometimes God teaches us the goodness of His ways even as we are in the process of obeying what He has revealed in Scripture. We are walking with Him. We know He is faithful. We do our best to trust and obey. Along the way, we discover that His ways are not only right but good—good for us. I wrote *Until Every Child Is Home* because I have seen that God's instruction for His people to care for orphans is not only what we should be doing because He said to and because we find needy kids across the globe, but also because by doing good for kids we are doing good for ourselves. I want local churches to see that by coming together to meet the needs of vulnerable kids, we advance our church ministries. Orphan care is strategic, compelling work, a means and not just a goal. Orphan care ministries do not suck the life out of a church—as some might think they would. Rather, foster-care, adoption, and support ministries enhance the general ministry of our local church.

In this book, I identify six spheres of ministry that benefit from a church's orphan-care work. Each chapter begins with the narrative of an individual or family who has expertise in helping us trace the ways that orphan-care ministries benefit not only vulnerable children but our churches as well. Then I unpack Scripture to help us better understand the focus God has for the church through orphan care. To facilitate group studies, each chapter concludes with a list of discussion and reflection questions.

In part 2, I write that by promoting foster care, adoption, and wrap-around support for families taking children into their homes, local churches develop theological depth. As Christians, we learn by reading Scripture, by hearing testimonies of other believers' experiences, and by putting into practice what we have read. You'll hear about the journeys of Douglas and Virginia Webster, Russell and Maria Moore, and Tate and Abby Williams. While God has worked in different ways in their specific foster and adoption journeys, each of these couples note that orphan care has helped them and their churches learn about God in ways they never had before. Old Testament references to God's concern for the orphan came alive for these couples as they became involved in foster care and adoption. I note how orphan-care ministry provides unique insight into passages from the Gospels and Paul's letters in the New Testament.

Part 3 surveys ways that foster-care and adoption ministries in a local church help the body to participate in the Great Commission. David and Heather Platt, Kent and Rosaria Butterfield, and Tony and Kimberly Merida exemplify our need to demonstrate concern for God's gospel among the nations and children. Here I walk us through passages from the Gospels, Acts, and Paul's letters to show that proclaiming gospel truth and personally caring for the vulnerable—like orphans—are not contrary pursuits. Rather, as we speak God's saving grace and open our homes to needy children, we obey the Great Commission to make disciples of all nations.

In the local church, I don't think we fully appreciate the

benefits orphan-care ministries bring us. And it's not just the blessings adoptive parents receive. These ministries provide incredible benefits to those who are *not* taking children into their homes as well. For every family who opens the front door to needy kids, multiple families are needed for support purposes. This is my concern in part 4. New Testament texts in Acts, 1 Corinthians, and Hebrews call members of the church to support and help one another in personal, sacrificial ways. Sometimes our churches fail to realize a deep sense of mutual commitment because we are not stepping out in ministries that stretch us to the point of realizing that we need one another. Foster care and adoption will do just that. The stories of Jason and Emily Johnson, Aaron and Mary Blake, and Bob and Kristen Miller display how foster-care and adoption initiatives provide unifying ministry opportunities for the whole body.

Racial conflict is one of the most pressing issues in contemporary Western culture. Sadly, the church has not consistently exemplified love to members of another race, even those sitting beside us on Sunday. Due to the disproportionately high number of minority children in foster care in the United States and the fact that many international adoptions are of children considered racial minorities in the States, churches called to foster and adopt can demonstrate the power of the gospel of Christ in combatting racial pride and injustice. In part 5, I tell how God has worked in and through John Mark and Angie Yeats, John and Terri Moore, and D. J. and Glorya Jordan to show the power of the gospel to humble and unify diverse races both in families and in local churches. And this is not a sub-theme for Christians. I note that key New Testament passages in Romans, Ephesians, and 1 Peter call the church to demonstrate racial unity before the watching world.

Writers are often surprised by what they learn when doing research for a book. What I learned while writing part 6, I wish I had never encountered. Though I have taken several classes and attended multiple conferences on fostering and adopting, I had not understood that pimps see the foster-care system as a supply chain for recruiting prostitutes. Interviewing Heidi Olson, Rhi Z (as I will call her), and Karen Countryman-Roswurm opened my eyes to the dark world of sex trafficking. As we Christians partner together to take in vulnerable kids and provide them with strong relational roots in the church, we disrupt the sex-trafficking pipeline. In this section, I show that Jesus' calls to compassion in the Gospels and Paul's exhortations to robust, enduring relationships in Ephesians compel us to intervene for the sake of these kids. (Note: though part 6 contains sensitive language, do not let this deter you from using it in group studies. Simply use words like *trafficking* or *abuse* for terms that you feel are inappropriate in a group setting or in the presence of children.)

"As the pastor, so the church" is not just a turn of phrase. This is a biblical idea. In part 7, I walk us through passages to note how Paul urges pastors to be examples for the churches under their care. Peter likewise calls pastors to exemplary leadership in 1 Peter 5. I then turn our attention to James 1:27: "Pure and undefiled religion in the sight of our God and Father is this: to visit orphans and widows in their distress, and to keep oneself unstained by the world." Who might James envision leading the church to care for the likes of orphans? To answer, I tell the stories of Jeff and Teresa Dodge, Kevin and Lynette Ezell, and Paul and Michelle Chitwood. In diverse situations, they have seen the power of pastoral leadership in orphan-care ministries.

That covers parts 2 through 7. Part 1? That is my story.

# Part 1

◆

# THE STRATEGIC PLACE OF ORPHAN CARE IN MY STORY

# 1

◆

# Born on the Right Side
# of History—Barely

My sister and I sat on the couch across from our parents. It was strange, to my six-year-old mind, that they had the same expression on their faces. They looked serious, concerned. I do not remember the exact words our parents spoke that afternoon as we sat in the '70s-décor living room with rust curtains and olive-green carpet, but the gist of the conversation was this: my sister and I were adopted.

I have no recollection of asking for details or feeling awkward about the news I had just heard, the news of my origin. "Some husbands and wives cannot have children at a hospital, so they can choose children whose parents are not able to help them," my parents explained. Fair enough. For me, it was back to playing football in the backyard and pestering my mom about second helpings of mashed potatoes at dinner.

Even during the fragile tween years, I was never insecure about being adopted. If the issue surfaced at school or in peer groups, I would interject briefly my own experience and move on. And God was gracious. Never was I the subject of teasing or scorn from peers because I came from Nebraska Children's Home and not from my parents' marital union. On a family trip in the autumn of 1984—the highlight of which was attending a home Nebraska Cornhuskers football game in Lincoln—we stopped in Omaha to visit the children's home. My parents had picked me up there thirteen years prior. I do not remember if it was on that trip or sometime later when I learned that my biological parents met in high school, one time, at a party. When my biological mom discovered she was pregnant, she was kicked out of the home. She found the hospitality of a physician in Omaha who took her in until I was born. She did light housework and helped care for his younger children as payment. There is no record that she told my biological father that I exist.

I have no scars from knowing I am adopted—but some kids do. They struggle to connect with their adoptive parents or siblings. They feel estranged or unwanted, a mistake (we will come back to this later). For me, the only scar of being adopted was that while I had such a good experience, many women were choosing to abort their babies when in situations similar to that of my biological mother. "That could have been me!" I would say to myself. I was born September 25, 1971. If I'd been born five hundred days later, when the landmark Supreme

> *If I'd been born five hundred days later, when the landmark Supreme Court decision Roe v. Wade was made, you would likely not be reading this book.*

Court decision *Roe v. Wade* was made, you would likely not be reading this book. The thought that aborted babies could have been adopted infuriated me when I was an adolescent and it still does today (more on that later, too). But my pro-life zeal is not just the result of personal reflection and gratitude that I was not aborted. I was born at a time in the history of the United States when children in the womb—even if unplanned by a man and a woman—were recognized as human beings who bear God's image. Scripture declares that people are made in God's image, redeemable through Jesus Christ.

## Created in God's Image

God's creative work in Genesis 1–2 climaxes with the creation of humanity—male and female created in the image of God. According to Genesis 1:26–30, one feature of image bearing is sharing responsibility for governing other animate creatures and plant life. There is a progressive flow in the creation account of Genesis 1. God's image bearers created on the sixth day are to care for and rule over plant life created on the third day (Gen. 1:9–13) and animal life created on the fifth day (Gen. 1:20–25). The creation story highlights God's interest in people. He likes them—us. He wants us to partner with Him in managing His creation.

And yet—by God's design—all is not well in creation. In Genesis 2:18, we see something that shocks us. God has been creating, and for the first time, He describes an element of creation as "not good." What is "not good"? The fact that Adam does not have a fellow image bearer to rule as God had intended in Genesis 1:26–30. Genesis 2:18–25 records that God creates image bearers with distinct genders so that through sexual union, image bearers produce more image bearers. Abortion militates against the very purposes of God in creation.

We see the importance of image bearing reproduction repeatedly throughout the entire Genesis narrative, in which God is recognized as sovereign over male and female bodies uniting to form offspring. The notion that human sexuality needs divine enablement in order to produce offspring is a major theme of Scripture. Childlessness is a crisis that forces Abraham and his descendants to trust God to provide them with children.[1] Abraham's lament to God concerning Sarah's barrenness in Genesis 15:1–6 provides the framework for how God would have His image bearers relate with Him: their reliance on Him (and ultimately His redemptive plan in Christ) is credited for righteousness (as the apostle Paul writes in Romans and Galatians).

Abraham's compromise to produce children with Hagar in Genesis 16 underscores the fact that without God's aid, Abraham and Sarah could not conceive a child. In Genesis 17, the Lord affirms that He will give Abraham and Sarah the ability to conceive—and will thus be known as the God who is powerful over life itself, jealous for image bearers.

We see this same issue with Isaac and Rebekah's situation as they tried to have children. No success. Rebekah is barren, and Isaac, the child of promise, cries out to the God of promise that his wife would be able to conceive (Gen. 25:21). Jacob, the son born to Isaac and Rebekah, knows that without God's creative work, no man and woman could conceive a child. When Jacob's wife Rachel complains to him, "Give me children, or else I die," Jacob replies, "Am I in the place of God?" (Gen. 30:1–2).

## Poems of Life

The importance of image bearing doesn't stop in the Genesis narrative. The Hebrew poetry of the Psalms includes the notion that human offspring—even while in the womb—are known by God. In Psalm 139:13–16, David wrote:

> For You formed my inward parts;
> You wove me in my mother's womb.
> I will give thanks to You, for I am fearfully and
>     wonderfully made;
> Wonderful are Your works,
> And my soul knows it very well.
> My frame was not hidden from You,
> When I was made in secret,
> And skillfully wrought in the depths of the earth;
> Your eyes have seen my unformed substance;
> And in Your book were all written
> The days that were ordained for me,
> When as yet there was not one of them.

Just beneath the surface of these poetic lines rests the idea that human reproduction is also God's creative activity. God is involved in the conception of each human life. He is jealous for the process of procreation because He is jealous to bear His image through humanity.

Throughout Psalm 139, David confesses God's all-encompassing, inescapable presence. He recounts God's knowledge of his paths, thoughts, and words and asks, "Where can I go from Your

Spirit? Or where can I flee from Your presence?" (v. 7). In Psalm 139:8–12 he raises a series of hypothetical situations that might challenge God's omniscience. But he refutes each. No location or condition is unknown to God. Because God knows every child in every womb, abortion contradicts God's purposes for humanity. I don't know if my birth mom knew God—but I know that God knew me even in her womb, and in even the womb I bore God's image.

When I think about God's purposes for my life, I think also of Psalm 8. Like Psalm 139, Psalm 8 is circular in its logic, concluding with an idea similar to where it begins. Psalm 8:1 and 9 read, "O LORD, our Lord, how majestic is Your name in all the earth!" (ESV). What prompts David to reflect on God's majesty? It appears that he had been meditating on God's creative work recorded in Genesis 1–2. In Psalm 8, he muses on the fact that God is powerful to create the moon and stars (v. 3), sheep, oxen, birds, and creatures of the sea (vv. 7–8). God's magnificence as Creator might lead to the conclusion that He would rule creation independently—a Being this great would need no assistance. But for David, God's majesty is seen in the fact that God created humanity as His image bearers to rule creation:

> When I consider Your heavens, the work of Your fingers,
> The moon and the stars, which You have ordained;
> What is man that You take thought of him,
> And the son of man that You care for him?
> Yet You have made him a little lower than God,
> And You crown him with glory and majesty!
> You make him to rule over the works of Your hands;
> You have put all things under his feet.

Though God is so great and could rule His creation without His image bearers, His majesty is expressed in His rule through them, through us, through children right now living in orphanages and foster homes, through children who secular society would think

> *His majesty is expressed in His rule . . . through children who secular society would think of as negotiable, in the crosshairs of "choice."*

of as negotiable, in the crosshairs of "choice." Though these children may have brought pain and anguish to their families, they have also brought joy and reward. In every instance, they have taught their parents about the glory of working with God to rule His creation. And in every instance, God wants to use them to teach us, His people, that same glory.

## Jesus, Born of a Woman

As I noted above, Abraham's *trust* in God's ability to provide him and Sarah a child becomes the biblical pattern for relating with God. In the storyline of Scripture, faith in Jesus Christ is the basis of right-standing with God. That is, faith in what Scripture records about Christ—including His birth as a human baby. The fact that God took up human flesh magnifies His interest in humanity—even those termed an unwanted pregnancy.

Consider what the New Testament states about Jesus' birth and the purposes of His life. The first chapter of Matthew begins with the genealogy of Jesus Christ and culminates with an account of His birth. Matthew 2 begins with the account of

Herod's decree to kill all male children under two years old in his attempt to eliminate Jesus in the process. Luke 2 likewise records the physical, human birth of Jesus as having come about according to the prophetic announcements of Luke 1. And the gospel of John begins with the statement that the Word was with God in the beginning and in time, "the Word became flesh, and dwelt among us" (John 1:14). At the outset of their narratives, three of the four New Testament Gospels note Jesus Christ's physical birth.

The New Testament Epistles then reflect on the implications of Jesus's birth. In Galatians 4:4, for example, Paul writes that at the pivotal moment in God's plan of redemption, "God sent forth His Son, born of a woman, born under the Law." Jesus bears the image of God not just as a human but as God's unique Son. The Son came as a man so that humanity could become sons of God. Though God created humanity in His image, human sin separates us from God. And New Testament writers like Paul describe Jesus as God's Son bearing God's image perfectly so that through His death and resurrection, we fallen image bearers could be reconciled to God. This is the gospel message—and it is based on the birth of a baby.

Ultimately, life in the womb has value because—as a human baby—the Son of God came to earth bearing God's image. Every life matters because of Jesus' life. Every life is redeemable by Him. With that knowledge, when we, the church, step into our role of caring for God's young image bearers, we participate with God in His plan to redeem His image bearers through Jesus. We participate in history-changing and eternity-shaping work. Much is at stake.

# DISCUSSION AND REFLECTION

- When you were a child or teen, did you know anyone who was adopted? How did adoption affect them?
- What would you say to a teen couple who found out they were expecting?
- What would you say to the parents of that couple?
- Read Psalms 8 and 139. How would you summarize the themes of human dignity and responsibility in these Psalms?
- In what ways does Jesus' incarnation affect your view of human dignity?
- As I mentioned in my story, had the timing of my birth been five hundred days later, I may not have survived. Have you ever thought that a person you know may not have been born? In what ways does that make you think differently about God's image-bearing stamp on all human life?

# 2

♦

# "We Want to Adopt You!"

Adoption has never been an "issue" for me, not something I dwelt on or perceived as a threat. Early in my relationship with Julie, who would become my wife, I told her that I was adopted, and she welcomed the news. Because of my positive experience and Scripture's clear teaching on the need to care for orphans, we discussed the possibility of one day adopting as well. Once we were married, however, those thoughts subsided as we had five biological children before our tenth anniversary in 2004.

The idea that we might expand our family through adoption didn't come up again until the summer of 2013, when we took a vacation to South Carolina. I'd recently reread the book of James and came upon this verse: "Pure and undefiled religion in the sight of our God and Father is this: to visit orphans and widows in their distress, and to keep oneself unstained by the world" (1:27). James's words stuck with me as I recalled Julie's and my premarital conversations about adopting. So I brought up the subject again with Julie, who willingly agreed.

Since most of our children were in their tween years, we

realized that for them it would be a major adjustment if we were to introduce new members into our family. I broached the subject while touring Charleston for a day when I announced that I was going to carry a heavy backpack, symbolizing a foster or adopted child. We would occasionally interrupt our sightseeing as if to change a diaper, give a bottle, or address some other need. We called the backpack "Mark" or "Molly," and throughout the day I considered the needs of the world and the resources of my family. It was a fun "experiment" and the kids all got into the adventure of it. But after vacation, we went back to the busyness of our lives and didn't give the idea more than a passing thought from time to time. As educational as our backpack adventure was, I had no idea that in the years to come, I would see just how truly needy orphans can be—how important it was for us to do more than just carry around a backpack and to step out in faith, and how much our family needed God's help to welcome kids into our home.

## Doors Closing, Doors Opening

That same summer when we were touring in Charleston, a prison inmate in central Missouri relinquished his parental rights of two biological daughters, Maggy and Molly.[1] His leadership and legal authority terminated, Maggy and Molly were at the mercy of other family members. The courts gave three different family members opportunity to care for the girls. All failed. By June 2013, they were without a forever family, orphans in the full custody of the state of Missouri.

While that was happening with Maggy and Molly, we had our own family change: our oldest child left for college, leaving us with an empty bedroom. Less than two weeks after our son's departure, Focus on the Family hosted a "Wait No More" informational meeting for pastors in our hometown of Kansas City. "Wait No More" events connect state social workers and children's advocacy agencies with that region's faith community in order to highlight children whose parents' parental rights have been terminated.

As a pastor in the area, I wanted to attend to see if there were ways our church could get involved. When Julie and I attended, however, the stories I heard became intensely personal. Being adopted, I felt a deeper connection to the kids who were profiled there. In every story, I read my own. The hallways of the event space were lined with photographs and details of kids who were in temporary foster homes or group facilities. Attendees slowly exited the conference area, mingling around the pictures and skimming the biographical information listed for these kids. As we exited the building and walked into the sunny August afternoon, neither Julie nor I could speak. We walked to our parking space in near silence, listening to God's call on our lives.

We went home and started looking for that backpack. Julie and I committed to praying daily for what God might have us do with our college son's bedroom. After a month of constant prayer, we approached our children about the circumstances the Lord was working in our minds. What we were considering would drastically change life for our four daughters still living at home. We needed information. Having heard of Russell Moore's *Adopted for Life,*[2] we purchased a copy and read it in a matter of days. We then passed it to our four girls and asked each of them to read it—and join us in seeking God's will.

The "Wait No More" event confirmed in Julie and me that we should pursue adoption ministry unless the Lord intervened and ceased our aspirations. Our children were, like us, naïve and scared but optimistic. Where to begin? Public and private adoption options abound. We chose to seek kids who were already in the foster-care system but whose parents' parental rights had been terminated—kids like those we had heard about at the "Wait No More" event.

## Ready, Set, Research

Like most parents, before we began the first foster licensing class, we had already begun to research. We discovered the sad reality of websites that coordinate and profile foster children whose parents' parental rights have been terminated. These children are under the care of the state, in foster homes, group homes, or residential facilities. On one of those websites (adoptuskids.org), we saw a profile that matched our interests. First, we wanted a sibling set. We feared if we took in one child, he or she would be overwhelmed at having so many older siblings. Second, we wanted girls. We were in the girl mode, having four eleven-to-sixteen-year-old girls still living in our home at the time. Third, we wanted a few years of space between our youngest biological child and the siblings we planned to adopt.

We thought if we could take a sibling set of girls who were younger than our biological daughters, these adopted girls would see the patterns of life and behavior in our older daughters as a model. We hoped that through these patterns, we could explain to the adopted girls that the good ways of life their new older sisters exhibited resulted from the good news of Jesus' life, death, and resurrection. The imagery of Psalms 127 and 128 was brewing in our minds. We understood that we needed to consider all children—even our adopted kids—a gift from the Lord as the psalmist writes in Psalm 127:3. I envisioned Psalm 128:3[3] taking place in my home as a table filled with children—girls, specifically—reflected God's goodness to one another while Julie and I looked on. Our strategy toward these ends was rooted in the principle of Titus 2, in which Paul described older women teaching younger women and older men teaching younger men. Our biological children would, in a sense, be a full generation emotionally and spiritually above their adopted siblings. We hoped that in time, the adopted girls would follow the model our biological daughters had established.

In January 2015, Julie and I saw Maggy and Molly on adoptuskids.org. They were five and six years old, respectively. We printed their photo and put it on our fridge. And with our biological daughters, we began praying daily for them. The patterns were starting to form.

We began our foster-care licensure class the next month, and by August we had completed our adoption licensure class as well. In the foster-care classes, while the curriculum covered the basics of parenting, it also dealt especially with behavioral and attachment issues that surface in 99.9 percent of kids in the foster-care system. We learned that the goal of the foster-care system is to reunify the children with their parent or parents once they have resolved to the court's satisfaction whatever issues gave rise to the children being removed from the home. So the foster class equipped foster parents to speak highly of and reinforce the biological parent-child bonds, even when the biological parents have blown it. This is tough stuff. As the social workers leading the

*The church—because of the power of the gospel—is strategically positioned to help kids who have had their world torn apart.*

class told story after story of difficulties that arise in foster care, some participants began to think twice about bringing kids into their homes. It was jarring for Julie and me at times too. But at some point during each class, the Holy Spirit brought Scripture to mind, specifically passages about the power of God to rework relationships through the gospel. I remembered what God had done in my life, what I preached every week. I was reminded of the power of the local church to provide identity and relational structure. During those class sessions, I became convinced that the church—because of the power of the gospel—is strategically positioned to help kids who have had their world torn apart. And we would definitely need the church's help.

## All Things New?

Like most newly licensed parents, we got right to it. The day we received our certificate in the mail, we contacted Maggy and Molly's caseworker to see if they had yet been adopted. We learned the girls had been living in a stable foster home for two years. Maggy and Molly's foster family had made sure the girls were in a school environment that could attend to their behavioral and learning challenges. They integrated the girls into their extended family. But with two biological children of their own and having already adopted one other child, they were unable to make the adoption commitment to the girls. The door was still open!

Over the next few months we spoke with the various members of the girls' care team. The school the girls attended was just as much a part of the girls' lives as the foster family. The school provided meals, social support, and love—even hiring an extra staff person to accompany one of the girls throughout the day to ensure she always had an emotionally stable adult with her. The school's commitment was genuine. (When we adopted the girls in November 2016, the principal and two teachers drove 250 miles round trip to celebrate with us—even though Maggy and Molly had been out of their school for eleven months.)

But the girls' caseworkers and counselors were the most stable network of relationships in Maggy's and Molly's lives. They intervened when the girls' biological family didn't follow court orders. They taught the girls the importance of truth and the horror of lies. They helped to emotionally connect the girls to our family. They gave the girls hope.

Visits to our home were filled with fear and excitement—themes that would characterize the first six months of Maggy's and Molly's lives with us. The first time the girls visited our home, in November 2015, one of the first activities we did with them was our Joshua rock basket. Joshua 4 records that when Joshua led the Israelites across the Jordan River, he had leaders of each of the twelve tribes take stones from the dry river bottom. Those stones were to be memorial stones for Israel, symbols of God's providence and power behind and before them. We have a basket of rocks on our fireplace, each numbered to a corresponding entry in a journal that recounts a particular blessing the Lord has worked in our lives. Patterns. The rock basket is an integral part of our family life, and we wanted to get to it straightaway with Maggy and Molly. Visits also included parks, arts and crafts, and activities purposed to connect Maggy and Molly with our biological daughters. We wanted Maggy and Molly to experience our patterns.

By the first week of December 2015, the caseworkers and therapist recommended to the judge presiding over Maggy and Molly's future that they should be placed in our home with a plan to adopt after six months. We moved the girls into our home on December 23. By Christmas Day we were already aware that the patterns of our family, however strong we thought they were, would be stretched to their limits if Maggy and Molly were to take our last name. The girls' anger and defiance surfaced seemingly out of the blue. At meals they would have burping contests and exhibit other bodily noises not welcome at the dinner table.

*What brought stability amid tantrums, anger, fear, hatred, biting, kicking, scratching, and sleepless nights? What kept us from giving up? Our local church.*

As Julie homeschooled them along with our biological daughters, Maggy and Molly would fight, distract, and defy. During family worship, the girls would wiggle, fidget uncontrollably, and throw the rocks from the Joshua basket. Maggy's and Molly's temper tantrums strained our patterns to the breaking point. When corrected or emotional, kids who have been abused exhibit physical strength beyond their years. When Julie confronted or corrected the girls, they bit, kicked, scratched, and hit her. And the walls of our home learned a new vocabulary along the way. After the girls had been with us for just one month, my already petite wife had lost considerable weight. Full nights of sleep had become a distant memory. While at work, I was constantly on edge that my wife would call with news of another blowup. Our four biological children felt threatened in their own home. What had we done?

Until the following summer, life was a roller-coaster for our biological family and Maggy and Molly. How did we manage? What brought stability amid tantrums, anger, fear, hatred, biting, kicking, scratching, and sleepless nights? What kept us from giving up? Our local church.

## DISCUSSION AND REFLECTION

- I carried a backpack around Charleston while on vacation to help my family visualize and experience what it might be like to have a foster or adopted child along with us. What tasks, activities, or games might help a family prepare for having a child with them?
- What do you know about the factors that lead social workers or police to remove children from their parents?
- How do these events affect the kids? How might knowledge of those situations affect foster or adoptive parents?

- Do you know anyone who has completed foster or adoption licenses? What did they share with you about that process?
- How might a church help a family during the transition phase when foster or adopted children are settling into their new home?

# 3

◆

# On Becoming a Funnel for God

I had been the teaching pastor of my church for fourteen years when I announced that my wife, Julie, and I were going to pursue foster-adopt ministry. Over the years, I had been open about being adopted. One tends to use his own life for illustrations—and since the New Testament references adoption (e.g., Rom. 8; Eph. 1:1–14)—telling my story helped folks connect the dots with Paul's statements.

The church committed to support us in any way necessary—and they did. When Maggy and Molly stayed with us for the first time, they went to church for the first time. The congregation handled them well, treating them just like any other guests. People didn't stare. When they spoke with the girls, they asked basic questions but didn't probe. It seemed like the church was as excited as we were about the expansion of our ministry! The church hosted a gift and toy shower and prayed with us for the day when the girls would move into our home. The church's enthusiastic support did not wane once the girls moved into our home—and that was when we really needed it.

Most foster or adoptive parents state that the first six months with the child or children are the most difficult. Everyone is in transition mode—and for many children, transitions bring to the surface fight-or-flight mechanisms. It would take two hands and all toes to count how often we called or texted church members pleading for prayer during the first six months Maggy and Molly were with us. So often we saw God's Spirit bring clarity and calmness to our home as a result of the church's prayers. Sometimes we would get texts or calls spontaneously as church members checked in on how things were going and told us they were praying for us.

But our church family did more than intercede in the crises. They developed relationships with the girls, creating emotional hooks the girls could grab hold of during the transition into our family. Parents of children in Maggy and Molly's Sunday school class made sure that Maggy and Molly were invited to all the social events and birthday parties. Older ladies in the church asked the girls to sit with them at fellowship meals. Younger ladies asked Maggy and Molly to help with general housekeeping items and clean-up after church events. It seemed like everyone wanted to engage the girls in conversation, weaving Maggy's and Molly's stories into the plot God was unfolding in our church family.

And the church was literally present when we celebrated the finalization of the adoption. The courtroom was packed—so packed that when our attorney was asking me a set of formal questions during the hearing, he extemporaneously motioned to the audience and said, "Can you assure the court that you will continue to give these children the kind of love you and your church are demonstrating here today?" I replied *yes* with a sense of conviction rare even for a pastor. In God's kind providence, a member of our church is a court reporter in our county. She took the day off work so she could sit in

> *The church hosted a gift and toy shower and prayed with us for the day when the girls would move into our home.*

the audience and watch the proceedings. In more ways than one she had an insider's perspective on the proceedings. She used her position to arrange for the judge—from the bench—to give Maggy and Molly gifts from our church. It is not every day that adopted kids get American Girl dolls from the man dressed in a black robe, the one everyone calls "Your Honor."

## The Church's Unique Capacity for All-Around Care

Yes, what took place in the courtroom was a made-for-TV scene, but it represents so much more. Our adopted daughters were able to see in our church how the gospel shapes relationships, engenders loving service, compassion, and humility. Because of what God has done to rescue believers, the church has the unique capacity to meet the spiritual, emotional, and social needs of orphans. The characteristics of the local church match the needs of orphans. Orphans have been lied to; the church is "the pillar and support of the truth" (1 Tim. 3:15). Orphans have wounds; the church is a "heart of compassion" (Col. 3:12). Orphans need instruction, and the church is the original worldview academy (Col. 3:16).

Since the adoption in November 2016, our church has continued to demonstrate the gospel to our daughters. At ladies' tea parties or social events, the girls are invited to participate just as our biological daughters participate. If our girls misbehave in Sunday school class, teachers offer loving correction in the same way they would correct other kids. Moms with toddlers invite our girls to help them walk their children around the foyer before and after services. When our girls host a party at our home, moms from church bring their children if they are able. Our church has been successful in helping us with our adopted girls because our church has been natural. God operates His rescue plan through real people being real.

## Every Church Cries, "Abba! Father!"

My positive adoption experience motivated my wife and me to consider adopting kids in the foster-care system. My church's genuine love for the needy and vulnerable established a safety net we knew we could rely on when times got tough. A third influence was the way New Testament writers described the gospel message; it just seemed to ring true with orphan-care ministries. I became convinced that God's plan to rescue humanity by delivering us from sin and the havoc it brings to relationships applies to the plight of kids in foster care or those needing a forever home.

At its core, the New Testament is God's revelation of Himself in Christ to forgive the sins of all people from all ethnicities. That my wife and I are Caucasian and our adopted girls are African American fits perfectly in how God created His church. God has established the church as a special, multiethnic people to display to the world what He has done for all of us. He rescues us from sin and calls us to join Him in rescuing the world. So the idea of orphan care (let's include foster care and both domestic and international adoption) is a ministry that squares with the macro themes of the New Testament—even when the word *adoption* is not used.

> *Because of what God has done to rescue believers, the church has the unique capacity to meet the spiritual, emotional, and social needs of orphans.*

In fact, the biblical concept of adoption was not invented by Paul. Paul employed it because it described what he was getting at: God's revelation of Himself in Christ forgiving the sins of people from all nations and by the Spirit bringing them together in the church to share what they have received. Christians are taken in by God, recipients of His hospitality, that we might extend hospitality to those in need. We are to be funnels.

With that understanding, studying what texts like the epistle to the Hebrews have to say about Christ motivated me to lead my family to begin caring for orphans. The author of Hebrews described Jesus' incarnation as a rescue mission: Jesus took up human flesh so that through His death He could defeat the one having the power of death—the devil—and freed those who all their lives were held captive by the fear of death (Heb. 2:14–15). For the author of Hebrews, Jesus' atoning self-sacrifice is the very act that defeated the devil, robbing him of power to enslave humanity in fear of final condemnation. Throughout the New Testament, God's work in Christ is in many ways summarized in that phrase, *rescue mission*.

Hebrews' portrayal of Christ parallels Paul's use of the

adoption metaphor. In Romans 8, Paul wrote that God's rescue plan in Christ justifies believers of their sin, bringing us into God's family: "You have not received a spirit of slavery leading to fear again, but you have received a spirit of adoption as sons by which we cry out, 'Abba! Father!'" (Rom. 8:15). Writing to the Galatian churches, Paul characterized himself and his Jewish kinsmen as those held in slavery by spiritual forces of oppression until the time when God sent His Son to redeem them. How did Paul describe this redemption? Adoption (Gal. 4:5). He told the Galatians believers, "Because you are sons, God has sent forth the Spirit of His Son into our hearts, crying, 'Abba! Father!'" (Gal. 4:6). To the Ephesians, Paul wrote that God planned from eternity to adopt believers into His family through Christ (Eph. 1:5).

The apostle John also described Christ's life, death, and resurrection as God's plan to rescue humanity from sin and the devil. In John 12, when Jesus approached Jerusalem for the final time, He told a crowd gathered around Him that the time for the judgment of the world had come, the time for the ruler of the world to be cast out (v. 31). John noted at the outset of the Upper Room Discourse (John 13–16) that the devil was active in persuading Judas to betray Jesus (John 13:2, 27). It was in this setting that Jesus stated that the love He demonstrated for the disciples should mark their commitment to one another (John 13:12–17, 34–35). In 1 John 3:16–17, the apostle wrote that God's love was manifested in the rescue mission of Christ's sacrificial death—which in turn is to be the motivation for believers to demonstrate love in all directions. In John's view, if we do not show love to the needy, we have no basis, no surety, that God's love abides in us.

The New Testament describes Christians as those who have

been adopted into God's family. We are called, forgiven, and welcomed. We address the God of creation and eternity as heavenly Father. So magnificent is our adoption that it is to flow out of us into the lives of the needy—such as vulnerable children in our neighborhoods and around the world. We are funnels, giving kids safe homes and the message of God's plan of adoption in Christ.

## Saved from Self-Righteousness

Adopting and fostering children is a noble task. And Julie and I would find it easy, as many other parents have, to dwell in self-righteousness over it all. "Look at what we are doing for the world! Look at how great we are! Someone owes us something! Maybe God should thank us!" Yet by adopting our daughters, Julie and I are merely giving what we have received from God. He has chosen and called us to be His adopted children. Adopting our daughters is a rational, natural response. Nothing special here. When we understand this biblical truth, it rescues us from feelings of self-righteousness that can too often surface in foster or adoptive parents.

Indeed, funnels receive and funnels release. Families and churches that work together to take in vulnerable kids are simply demonstrating what God has done for us in Christ. The author of Hebrews and the apostles Paul and John want us to understand that concept. As does James. James 1:27 describes what that demonstration looks like: that we care for orphans. James says that is the way to pure and undefiled religion. What does he mean? Religion that works like a funnel.

As a result of adopting our daughters, Julie and I have a greater appreciation for our adoption into God's family. When we are frustrated by their occasional disobedience and apparent lack of gratitude for what we have done for them, God gently reminds us of our lack of appreciation for what He has done in our lives. When we see reports of kids aging out of the foster-care system only to enter into a life of crime or hear of a child prostitution ring populated by foster kids—knowing that our daughters could have ended up in either scenario—we are mindful that giving what we have received really does make a difference.

## DISCUSSION AND REFLECTION

- How have you seen Christians react when someone in the church began fostering or adopting children?
- How might Sunday school classes or church small groups prepare for ministering to children who have endured trauma? In what ways can they help these kids transition into the church community?
- Read Romans 8 and Ephesians 1:1–14. In what ways is orphan care an expression of New Testament Christianity?
- How might the biblical texts noted in this chapter guard us from feelings of self-righteousness as we engage in ministries like orphan care?
- As you think about our call as funnels and rescue workers, what are some steps you can take to demonstrate the reality of Christ's death and resurrection to orphans and their foster or adopted families?

# Part 2

◆

# GOD'S STRATEGY FOR ORPHAN CARE:

## Working Through We Who Have Experienced His Care

# 4

## How Many First-Born Children Can a Couple Have?

Doug and Virginia Webster adopted two children for twelve dollars. You may know someone who spent tens of thousands of dollars to adopt—or perhaps you did!

In the early 1980s, the Websters were living in Canada while Doug attended graduate school at the University of Toronto. The Websters adopted their oldest son, Andrew, from the Toronto Children's Aid Society and their younger son, Jeremiah, from a Christian adoption agency. The only cost they paid was a small licensing fee, plus seven dollars for the oldest and five dollars for their younger son.

"When I tell people we paid seven dollars for Jeremiah and five dollars for Andrew, they're shocked at first and then impressed by the Canadian government's insistence on money not being a factor in adoption," Doug told me.

Though the Websters thought they would not be able to have children, they still had a great desire to be parents. "Looking back, I find it amazing that we actually took the initiative,

filled out all the paperwork for several adoption agencies, and
did the interviews, physicals, and home study," Doug said.

Even though Virginia was working two jobs while Doug was
a full-time student, they were poor even by graduate-student
standards. They lived in a one-bedroom apartment, not even
an office to spare. "Who in their right mind, in the middle of a
pressured, over-worked schedule, decides to pursue adoption?"
Doug said, joking. "I chalk it up to the gracious providence of
God, not to our good judgment. God took the initiative so we
would take the initiative. In retrospect, I see that is how life is
supposed to work."

The Websters' church in Toronto had small community
groups that met weekly for prayer and Bible study, so even
though they didn't want to make a big deal about pursuing adoption, they did ask their group and extended family to pray about
their situation. "We had no idea how long the process might
take, and we thought it best to rely on the prayers and love of our
extended family in the States," he said.

Within a year, God began to answer their prayers. The Websters were able to pick up Andrew at Women's College Hospital
in downtown Toronto within twenty-four hours of his birth.
Jeremiah was born in Ottawa, Canada, and arrived in Toronto
for the Websters to bring home within seven days of his birth.
"We had the privilege of essentially parenting both of our boys
from the beginning," Doug shared.

Doug and Virginia were able to parent a girl from the beginning as well. In the Lord's providence, Virginia gave birth to a
daughter a few years after the Websters had adopted their boys.
"The birth of our daughter confirmed to us that there was no
real difference between adoption and conception when it came

to our sons and daughter. It really did not make a difference," Doug said. Although he admitted that the boys enjoyed some good-natured kidding at their daughter's expense. "Our boys teased their sister, saying, 'We're special. We were chosen! You just came along!'"

As Andrew and Jeremiah grew, Doug and Virginia were open to them about the fact that they were adopted, though they weren't sure exactly how much the boys could grasp the concept. They found out one Toronto winter day when the snow was deep. Virginia was bringing the boys home from taking them shopping with her. The boys were six and four years old, and Virginia was pregnant with their daughter. Suddenly, in this snowy scene, Jeremiah plopped his bag down in the snow and announced, "I don't have to carry this, I'm adopted!" Virginia had never heard her son use the word *adopted*, so she was perplexed, stunned, and unsure of what to say. Turns out, she did not have to say anything. Andrew told his brother, "Adopted or not, pick it up!" Four-year-old Jeremiah picked up his bag and they trudged home.

As an adult, Jeremiah began to inquire about his biological history. Doug and Virginia fully supported his quest. He was able to locate his biological mother and meet her. The process of being adopted led him to contribute to and edit a book titled *The Spirit of Adoption*.[1]

Doug and Virginia cherish each of their children. Three children united as siblings in one family but all with different genes. All unique, beautiful. "As it turned out," Doug said, "all three of our children are firstborn, which is how I think the sons and daughters of God are privileged in the gospel of the kingdom." What gives Doug and Virginia this perspective?

What the Scriptures state about God's care for orphans. Both the Old and New Testaments repeatedly describe God as personally concerned for the vulnerable—like orphans—and He desires for everyone, including the least of these, to be privileged sons and daughters in His kingdom. This is why James 1:27 is such a strong command: if we want to offer pure and undefiled lives of faith to God, then we must be concerned about caring for orphans.

## The God Who Cares and Calls His People to Care Too

Indeed, both Old and New Testament writers described God's care for those on the margins of society. "When you read the Bible," David Platt wrote in *Counter Culture*, "you see over and over God's passion to demonstrate his power and love in the life of the orphan."[2] In Deuteronomy 10, Moses exhorted Israel to remember not only their privileged status in God's redemptive plan but also to remember God's personal concern for the orphans among them (vv. 10:18–19). Psalm 10 places God's concern for the orphan as a means of describing His care for all who are oppressed. Even though the arrogant scheme and carry out injustice, the psalmist prayed, "The unfortunate commits himself to You; You have been the helper of the orphan" (v. 14). In Psalm 68, David described God as so powerful that He is a father to the fatherless and a judge (a rescuer) for widows (v. 5). David Prince, pastor of Ashland Avenue Baptist Church in Lexington, Kentucky, and assistant professor of preaching at The Southern Baptist Theological Seminary, commented that "this is the vision of pure religion He [God] places before us to reflect Him to the world as fathers to the fatherless."[3] The Old Testament prophet Jeremiah prophesied against the nation of Edom, the descendants of Esau, saying that God would care for the orphan and widow even when foreign nations came to invade them (Jer. 49:11). Hosea prophesied similarly, seeing in God's concern for the orphan a basis of hope that God would care for Israel despite the threat of foreign invasion (Hos. 14:3). Whether concerning foreign nations or Israel, the prophets of Israel wanted the people to understand God's eye toward the vulnerable.

But it isn't enough for God's people simply to understand that part of God's care. Throughout Scripture, God's personal concern for the marginalized serves as the motivation for His people to join Him in caring for the orphans among them. This is God's strategy for orphan care. In Deuteronomy 14:29, Moses commanded Israel to provide for the orphan just as they would the Levites who had no portion of land. Moses commanded Israel that when they celebrated national festivals, they were to include orphans (Deut. 16:11, 14).

During harvest, Israel was instructed to leave portions in their fields that those like the orphans could come and find provision from God's bounty (Deut. 24:19–21). But Moses commanded not only that the Israelites leave in their fields a portion for the needy but also that they regularly bring a portion of their profits to support those like the orphans who had no means of income (Deut. 26:12).

Old Testament prophets like Isaiah and Jeremiah echoed Moses's commands for Israel to care for the orphans among them, even heightening the severity of consequences if Israel would refuse to treat the vulnerable the way that God had treated them. For Isaiah and Jeremiah, Israel's fidelity to the orphan-care commands served as a litmus test for Israel's faithfulness to God. Isaiah began his prophesy by indicting Israel of their sinful ways and calling the nation to repent. What would repentance look like? In part, to practice orphan care: "Learn to do good; seek justice, reprove the ruthless, defend the orphan, plead for the widow" (Isa. 1:17). Israel's leaders were in Isaiah's crosshairs: "Everyone loves a bribe and chases after rewards. They do not defend the orphan, nor does the widow's plea come before them" (Isa. 1:23). Many in Jeremiah's day thought themselves safe because the temple yet stood in Jerusalem. However, according to Jeremiah, the fact that God's people prospered while the orphan and needy among them continued in desperation was evidence that Judah no longer reverenced the Lord (Jer. 7:1–8). Jeremiah was as concerned for the orphan as he was the state of the temple, prophesying that unless the people of Judah took up causes like justice for the orphan, God would come and remove not only the temple from Jerusalem, but them from the land!

*God's personal concern for the marginalized serves as the motivation for His people to join Him in caring for the orphans among them. This is God's strategy for orphan care.*

Tracing God's concern for orphans and His call to His people to join Him in caring for the needy establishes an accurate perspective for understanding James's statement that pure and undefiled religion includes orphan care (James 1:27). Not just for the people of biblical times, but for us today. God's plan to care for the vulnerable, like orphans, is to work through you and me, with the support of our churches, to foster and adopt children whose biological parents are unwilling or unable to fulfill their parental roles.

## Parenting and the Love of God

Scripture's portrait of God as one who personally cares for kids who are right now in orphanages and foster homes serves as a sure foundation for our interest in orphan care today. Doug and Virginia Webster did not sign up for adoption to save the world one child at a time. They just wanted to have children. But as Christians, their parenting became an expression of God's love. They exhibited God's love to their boys before their daughter was born and each day since. Referring to the local church's efforts to encourage foster care and adoption, Doug commented that "this ministry cannot become a program that is managed and marketed. Children are not problems to be fixed but opportunities to show God's love. The bottom line is this: children are needy. They are fully dependent on others, and that is why Jesus made them His priority."

Doug and Virginia's story is a beautiful example of how we can take up God's mission to care for orphans. "The Lord turns everything upside down," Doug said. "The people who deserve our attention are on the bottom, not the top. Normal adult issues, sensitivities, problems, and priorities pale in comparison to welcoming and nurturing these little ones for Christ and His kingdom." As we partner with our local church to care for kids in crisis, we participate in God's concern for His glory in His image bearers. Every human is unique, all are first-born of God.

# DISCUSSION AND REFLECTION

- Of the Old Testament passages cited in this chapter, which most impact you? Why?
- Why would God place such a priority on orphan care throughout the various writings of the Old Testament?
- Have you known couples who experienced infertility? In what ways did they respond? How might you and your church spiritually support couples who are unable to have biological children?
- The Websters paid less to adopt than many of us pay for coffee. Have you known couples who struggled to pay for an adoption? How might you and your church help them financially?
- What dangers might result if you were to treat your biological, foster, or adopted children differently? What safeguards might you put in place to be sure that you parent each according to their individual needs while at the same creating an atmosphere of equity in your home?

# 5

---

# What Does Spiritual Warfare Have to Do with Orphan Care?

Early in their marriage, Russell Moore and his wife, Maria, were unable to have biological children. Maria was open to starting a family through adoption but Russell was hesitant, wanting to fulfill his dream of having "children of his own." The frustration of infertility led the Moores to seek counsel and prayer from friends. Slowly Russell became open to the idea of adoption—an idea he had read in Scripture and preached from the pulpit. So Russell and Maria adopted two boys from a Russian orphanage.

Although Russell had preached and lectured through the New Testament books of Romans, Galatians, and Ephesians, he did not truly understand the theological reality of adoption until he held his no-longer-orphan sons in his arms.[1] With his deeper and more profound perspective, Russell, pastor, seminary professor, and president of the Ethics and Religious Liberty Commission (ERLC[2]), was determined to make it part of his mission to broaden the church's understanding of caring for vulnerable kids.

In *Adopted for Life,* Russell wrote that "Christians ought to lead in the area of adoption, since we have a theological grounding in the doctrine of adoption."[3] To back up his point, he included a Scripture index in his book; it includes thirty-four references from Genesis alone. Romans is referenced fifty times, and Galatians thirty times. But orphan care isn't just about a romantic and charitable concept for Christians. Russell cites, rightfully so, that orphan care is about engaging in spiritual warfare.

> Adoption is hard and will take everything you have, but it's worth it. The calling to care for widows and orphans is a mission that is about more than charity. It's about spiritual warfare, and it requires grit and courage.[4]

Why did he use a term like *warfare?* Especially when readers might understand these to provoke violence. Russell explained it to me this way: "Because the New Testament puts the entirety of the Christian's life in the context of spiritual warfare, particularly as it relates to children. The entire canon of Scripture sees the emergence of life as a threat to the principalities and powers. From Genesis to Revelation, children are at the crosshairs of a fallen universe." This is like *Star Wars.* As we go about our daily lives, we are in the midst of a cosmic battle as the devil and his forces seek to destroy God's image bearers and rob God of glory. Orphans are easy prey for the devil. As our churches engage in foster-care and adoption ministries, you and I join God in the spiritual battle of being jealous for His image in the lives of vulnerable kids.

## Unexpected War Cries
## of God's Greatness

Since God has created man in His image, it follows that God's enemy would seek to destroy life. The devil's chief strategy is to ruin relationships by separating people from God and one another. His strategy has not changed since Genesis 3, in which he deceived Eve to sow discord between God and His image bearers, the first human family. From Genesis 3 onward, the Bible is a story of spiritual warfare.

In chapter 1 of this book, I discussed the way Psalm 8 presents the value of life. As God's image bearers, humans participate with God to manage His creation. But Psalm 8 also presents spiritual warfare imagery. In this psalm, David wrote that God demonstrates His warrior power even through the cries of an infant: "From the mouth of infants and nursing babes You have established strength because of Your adversaries, to make the enemy and the revengeful cease" (v. 2). In the psalmist's mind, suckling children and the sounds of a church nursery are war cries of God's greatness. How so? God is the Creator of life, accomplishing a feat that none of His foes could replicate. Since

> *In the psalmist's mind, suckling children and the sounds of a church nursery are war cries of God's greatness.*

babies bear the image of God, even the cry of a baby shuts the mouths of any boastful opponents exalting themselves in God's presence. David used the ironic picture of a crying child—not an image of power in our day or his—to present God's power as Creator.

Scenes of spiritual warfare also surface through Jesus' ministry in the Gospels. Matthew 12:22–30, Mark 3:22–27, and Luke 11:14–23 all record the Jewish leadership's attempt to discredit Jesus by telling the crowds that Jesus' miraculous power had demonic origin. In Luke 11:14–23, Jesus healed a demon-possessed man who had been unable to speak. After Jesus healed the man, the crowds were astounded at His supernatural ability. But some in the crowd, likely Pharisees and scribes, stated that Beelzebul, the devil, gave Jesus His power. Jesus called them out for foolishness: "If Satan also is divided against himself, how will his kingdom stand?" (Luke 11:18). The comments of those who questioned Jesus opened a window of opportunity for Jesus to teach about His mission—and He did so in Luke 11:21–22 using terms of conquest and warfare. Jesus described Satan as a powerful figure, having dominion over a kingdom. Satan is fully armed, guarding his possessions so his rule might endure. How could such a leader be overthrown? Jesus answered with a simple battle strategy: "When someone stronger than he attacks him and overpowers him, he takes away from him all his armor on which he had relied and distributes his plunder" (Luke 11:22). What might Jesus mean by "plunder"? What would Jesus, the stronger man, plunder from Satan's kingdom? People, God's image bearers—kids in foster homes and orphanages around the world who are God's treasures, those He wants to redeem through Jesus Christ and our care.

The apostle Paul wrote about this great cosmic battle in both Colossians and Ephesians. When God saves a person, Paul wrote in Colossians 1:13–14 and 2:15, they are transferred from the kingdom of darkness into the kingdom of God's beloved Son. Because the believer's sins are forgiven, Satan is disarmed of a list he might use to accuse the believer before God. Paul explained that because of Christ's death and resurrection, the roles of the believer and Satan have been reversed. Satan aims to accuse the believer and shame him or her before God, but Christ shamed Satan by triumphing over him on the cross.

In Ephesians 1:18–21, Paul wrote that God showed His power by raising Christ from the dead and sitting Christ at His right hand—the place of authority—in the heavens. Jesus thus sits "far above all rule and authority and power and dominion, and every name that is named, not only in this age but also in the one to come" (v. 21). Jesus' victorious death and resurrection are decisive moments in the scriptural storyline of spiritual warfare. Since Jesus plundered Satan's kingdom, the spoils of war Jesus takes from him are recognized as God's glorious inheritance.

In Ephesians 2:1–5, Paul reflected on God's battle plan against Satan. Though Satan militates against God by causing God's image bearers to walk in sin and rebellion against their Creator, God intervenes by showing His great mercy and grace. God rescues His people from Satan's scheming power "so that in the ages to come He might show the surpassing riches of His grace in kindness toward us in Christ Jesus" (Eph. 2:7). God wants His enemies to see that He is not only the God of physical life but the God who makes the spiritually dead come alive and live in the church. Believers assembled together in the church are God's trophy of victory.

In Ephesians 3:10, Paul wrote that through the church God displays His wisdom "to the rulers and the authorities in the heavenly places." In Ephesians, to speak of the cosmos is to speak of the abode of God's opponents, the spiritual forces of Satan. Orphan care—like any missions or evangelistic ministry that builds the church—is a distinctly spiritual endeavor. Russell explained it this way: "A pastor's preaching on the cosmic and missional aspects of adoption will not come back void."[5]

Satan has attacked God's unique image bearers since the garden of Eden, and the result has always been the breakdown of relationships. Children are the victims of the devil's schemes. This is why orphan care is warfare. God draws the weak and vulnerable to Christ for salvation that God would display His greatness in the church. By caring for orphans, believers participate in God's battle against Satan. We are doing for children what God has done for us. Our work in orphan care does not guarantee that children will embrace Christianity—though we pray God would forgive their sins and give them new spiritual life in Christ. We care for orphans because we know what it is like to be cared for when we were in the crosshairs of the spiritual battle, dominated by Satan's lies and living in darkness. In our vulnerable state, God went to battle for us in Christ. Orphan care is giving what we have received.

"That is one of the reasons we are called to care for the vulnerable in their distress," Russell told me. "They are not just a benevolence project. This world is not the way it is supposed to be, and so we are called to speak a different word against that."

## Loving as We Have Been Loved

Russell has seen firsthand how orphan care affects the church. "Evangelicals who become involved in orphan care become involved in the full range of concerns about love of neighbor," he told me. "There are so many intersections between various forms of ministry." He offered an example of a church in Alabama that was segregated for generations under the influence of Jim Crow laws. "The church was thus largely apathetic to racial justice issues," Russell said. "This was until families in the church started adopting, and then parents who previously were unmoved by racial concerns were suddenly facing issues with their own children that prompted the congregation to become aware of the need for racial reconciliation."

And neighborly love is always an expression of the Great Commission. If our churches are going to be successful in foster-care and adoption ministries, we will have to see them as a vital part of our broader concern for making disciples of all nations. A surefire way to divide a church is to make orphan care a litmus test for belonging. Seeing Christianity as concerned for orphan care and nothing else will lead us to a place of spiritual darkness. We do our best work when we view the kids in our neighborhoods and in orphanages around the world within the scope of God's concern for disciples from every people and nation. Foster care and adoption enhance the Great Commission culture of our churches, contributing to our sense of mission, fulfilling it. That's why orphan care is strategic work, benefiting kids and churches.

Orphan care not only helps our church's sense of mission, it helps us know God. In his book, Russell reflected on wearing a plastic hat at one of his adopted son's birthday parties. "It's my theologian's cap; it's taught me far more about my God and his gospel than the tasseled formal scholar's hat on my shelf ever has."[6] At its core, orphan care provides believers the opportunity to learn of God and reflect Him to needy children. While we enjoy watching *Star Wars* and its battles, we are fighting the real dark side. Here we join our warrior God in His battle for glory on earth reflected even to the heavens.

◆

## DISCUSSION AND REFLECTION

- Russell Moore knew the theological theme of adoption in Scripture but did not fully grasp it until he and Maria adopted their sons. Have you known foster or adoptive parents who have made similar statements? In what ways did the process of caring for orphans deepen their understanding of the gospel?
- In your experience, what characterizes churches that emphasize orphan-care ministries?
- Read Luke 11:14–23 and Ephesians 1:15–23. What ideas connect these passages?
- How would your church's orphan-care ministry be an act of spiritual warfare?

# 6

## Taking a Jet Plane
## into the Earthquake Zone

Tate Williams was remodeling a kitchen in Cedar City, Utah, on the morning of Thursday, January 14, 2010. He had seen reports of a massive earthquake that rocked Haiti two days before. The quake measured 7.0 on the catastrophic magnitude scale, affecting millions and claiming tens of thousands of lives. "It was a crisis moment for me—a fork in the road," he told me. "The news images were so raw, and I couldn't shake them."

Tate had been working for his brother, remodeling houses in Cedar City for a couple years. Having graduated from Wheaton College in 2007, Tate was unsure how his degree in applied health science would fit into God's plan for his life. Remodeling homes seemed the right way to wait on the Lord. And the Lord called that morning when Tate heard the news of the earthquake.

While he was living in Cedar City, a deacon from his church began to disciple him. This deacon worked as a janitor at a local college. He used his position to meet students and engage in campus ministry, inviting them to Bible studies at the church.

He invited Tate, too, and asked Tate to lead the study. "That was this deacon's form of discipleship!" Tate shared with a chuckle. "This was a time of deepening my knowledge of God and how much He loved me."

God was bringing His personal work in Tate's life to the surface of Tate's conscience and broadening Tate's horizons for personal involvement in the lives of the needy. During the months prior to January 2010, the Bible study he led went chronologically through the life of Christ. Even as the study progressed, Jesus' Sermon on the Mount in Matthew 5–7 would not leave him alone. "My whole life got unraveled," he said. He began to understand the kingdom of God as a relational dynamic. "Up 'til then, I had only had this socialization into church culture."

But Tate remembers the summer and fall of 2009 for other reasons too. He and his girlfriend, Abby, got engaged in August. Whatever God was doing in Tate's life, Abby would participate also. Tate began to understand more personally that enjoying God's kingdom was directly related to sharing the message of the kingdom with all of one's life. What God had given to those in Jesus' kingdom was not for them to horde but for them to give away—and the only way for them to truly enjoy the kingdom was, ironically, to pass it along.

"The kingdom calls the church to engage in mission, to engage the marginalized. These passages in the Gospels began to inform a growing desire to be sensitive to the needs of the world," Tate recalled of that formative period at the end of 2009. "I was recognizing that following Jesus meant being willing to sell it all and go all-in in practical ways."

That Thursday morning in January as Tate was remodeling trim work above a refrigerator at a home in Cedar City, Utah, the Lord impressed on Tate, *Go!* "It was what the older folks call 'unction,'" Tate said. "I was not under duress, but it felt like an either-or moment." Tate had to count the cost. With Abby in graduate school in Kansas, planning their May 2010 wedding in her spare moments, could Tate step away from a stable income and proximity to Abby to carry out God's call in Haiti?

Through social media, Tate contacted a friend who had posted about going to Haiti to help victims. Tate's friend shared of the immediate need for workers to coordinate the relief effort. Tate reached out to his pastor to share the burden God had put on Tate's mind. That day the church liquidated its mission budget, and the next morning the church had a three thousand dollar check for Tate to get to Haiti. In God's providence, the following day Tate boarded a private flight from Las Vegas to Santa Domingo. Tate and Abby's story illustrates that God may call us to what seems a radical change of life in order to care for vulnerable kids. But doesn't Jesus call His disciples to trusting Him fully, from the heart?

## The Inside-Out, Upside-Down Kingdom of God

In Jesus' Sermon on the Mount (Matt. 5–7), He establishes a framework of beliefs and behavior for His disciples and the crowds gathering about Him. As Tate observed in his studies, Jesus called those who would participate in the kingdom to consider its value and respond appropriately. The response Jesus calls for? Inside-out, upside-down righteousness.

Matthew 5 lists Jesus' critique of the Jewish elite's religious pretense and posturing to use God for their own status. Jesus said that the blessed ones of the kingdom are poor in spirit. They mourn their sin while longing for righteousness. They are gentle, merciful, and pure in heart. Their inverted way of living makes them stand out like a city on a hill and a lamp on a lampstand. Perhaps no pattern of life so illuminates the lives of those in the kingdom of God as love—even for our enemies. Perfect righteousness, Jesus said, inverts the world's ways of thinking as it orients life to God from the heart.

In the Sermon on the Mount, Jesus emphasized authentic spirituality in every sphere of life—even in our resources. Jesus stated that a lifestyle of radical generosity results from a robust faith in God's faithfulness to provide. He exhorted His followers to avoid the trap of amassing worldly wealth, where it will decay or perhaps get stolen. Instead, He told those who would participate in God's kingdom, "Store up for yourselves treasures in heaven, where neither moth nor rust destroys, and where thieves do not break in or steal" (Matt. 6:20). In Luke 6:20–49, He also emphasized the spiritual danger of accumulating wealth while ignoring the needs of those around us. Jesus went so far as to pronounce woes on those who are rich, comfortable, and uncaring.

How should Jesus' disciples act to those in need? Give to those who ask from us, lend to them, and be merciful just as the Father is merciful.[1] In *Jesus and the Gospels,* New Testament scholar Craig L. Blomberg wrote that in light of Luke's emphasis on generosity, Luke may have been writing to a Christian audience that was better off than some other groups around them.[2] So when Tate called his friend who was urgently doing earthquake relief in Haiti, he was just taking Jesus at His word.

What resources might the disciple rely on if their generosity would threaten their security and savings? The generous eye of the heavenly Father. Tate's parents had instilled in him and his siblings that God is pleased to meet the needs of His people as they rely on Him. "A big part of my childhood was being groomed for a lifestyle of faith," he said. "A lifestyle that said, 'Yes, planning,' and 'Yes, strategy,' but also, 'Yes, trust,' and 'Yes, radical belief that God does, in fact, control all things.'"[3] The center point of the Sermon on the Mount is in Matthew 6:25–34 with Jesus' portrayal of the Father's generous care—for even the lilies of the field. What should Jesus' disciples do when they become anxious over the needs of life—like food, drink, and clothing? "Seek first His kingdom and His righteousness, and all these things will be added to you" (Matt. 6:33). In his book *Sermon on the Mount*, author Scot McKnight wrote, "Those who are unwilling to see the hand of God in providence and trust the caring Father for the necessities of life are called 'you of little faith,' a term in Matthew for faith failure, that is, those living between faithful discipleship and unbelief (8:26; 14:31; 16:8; 17:20)."[4] That is it. We who have experienced the care of the heavenly Father are compelled to care because we know we can rely on Him in the future.

> *What resources might the disciple rely on if their generosity would threaten their security and savings? The generous eye of the heavenly Father.*

## Remodeling Families

During Tate and Abby's premarital counseling, they discussed what they believed God had for them together. They both sensed a desire to adopt children and to be involved in missions, even internationally, in some way. Many couples wait until later in life to think about fully surrendering to God. Not Tate and Abby. And they set an example for all the church.

Tate's response of faith in June 2010 instigated a change in the whole course of Tate and Abby's lives. Right after the earthquake struck, Tate's friend, whom he had contacted through social media, was helping with logistics for The Global Orphan Project (GOProject), transporting goods from the Dominican Republic to Haiti. Tate joined him, serving in Haiti for two months. Along the way, Tate became close friends with the leadership of GOProject. In April 2010, the CEO of GOProject invited Tate to join their staff, initially helping with the efforts in Haiti a couple of weeks each month. Tate took the job.

Tate has served with GOProject in various capacities, most recently helping churches to care for vulnerable kids in their communities through a program called Care Portal. Care Portal allows social workers in the children's division of participating states to broadcast needs in specific families. Local churches in the zip code of these needy kids and families receive an e-mail containing the specifics of the situation and how the church might partner to meet the need. Care Portal provides churches the opportunity to keep families together, help establish foster kids in new families, and meet the needs of newly adopted children. So Tate has gone from remodeling homes to remodeling families.

As for remodeling his own family? Tate and Abby married as planned in May 2010. Together he and Abby have one biological child and three children adopted out of foster care in the United States.

As in Tate's case, God used a world crisis to get his attention. He may do the same for you and me. Or perhaps He will use a personal crisis, like infertility. These are moments when God reminds us of His faithfulness and bids us to follow Him from the inside out. If we take that radical step, we can be assured of His leadership along the way.

---

## DISCUSSION AND REFLECTION

- Have you known someone who had such a sense of God's call on their life at a particular time that they felt they had to make a radical change in order to obey? What were the results of their faithfulness?
- God used a deacon in Tate's church to teach him of authentic discipleship. How is being discipled in a local church helpful preparation for fostering or adopting needy children?
- In what ways are children particularly vulnerable during natural disasters and tragedies of various kinds?
- Tate's study of Jesus' teaching sensitized him to God's call to Haiti. What passage or passages from the Sermon on the Mount (Matt. 5–7) most impact you? How so?

- How might spouses help each other respond to God's call to foster or adopt?
- Might God be using a crisis to get your attention regarding orphan care? In what ways is God leading you to respond?

# Part 3

◆

## ORPHAN CARE AND THE GREAT COMMISSION

# 7

# How Many Continents Can You Get into One House?

Early in David and Heather Platt's marriage, they were unable to conceive a child naturally. So they decided to pursue adoption. After more than a year of research, paperwork, and physical exams, they traveled to Kazakhstan in hopes of adopting a baby boy whose parents had abandoned him.

At the time, David was pastoring The Church at Brook Hills in Birmingham, Alabama, so he and Heather took some time away from their church to travel to the orphanage in Kazakhstan, which was called a "baby house." Twice a day for two weeks, David and Heather had one-hour visits with the boy they hoped would be their first son. While there, the Platts learned that most adoptive parents don't visit the baby house, as they had. Many parents fill out the paperwork and then show up for the court hearing, finalizing the adoption. But David and Heather wanted to bond with their child and spend as much time with him as they could—even though it would stretch them emotionally and financially. "We learned pretty quickly that orphans are easier to forget if you don't see their faces," David wrote in *Counter Culture*. "They're easier to ignore if you don't know their names. They're easier to overlook if you don't hold them in your arms."

Finally, after seventeen months, the Platts' adoption journey was completed, and they were able to bring their son home. Within two weeks of arriving home with their newly adopted son, Heather found out she was expecting. "I have no doubt that divine prerogative is the only explanation behind why Heather got pregnant when she did," David wrote. "God clearly had something more glorious in mind as he used this hardship in our lives to lead us to adopt a precious little boy in an obscure city of northwestern Kazakhstan whom we would never have met otherwise."[1]

God had begun a work in their hearts, and they sought to adopt again. "God had opened our eyes to the needs of the orphan, and an adoption process that began as a desire to fill a void in our hearts became a desire to reflect a reality in God's [heart]," David wrote.[2] This time they adopted a girl from China. As an infant, she was abandoned in a paper box outside an orphanage. Now she receives the tangible loving care of parents, brothers, and a heavenly Father.

The Platts learned quickly that orphan care is an expression of the Great Commission, a physical, tangible way to demonstrate personally the spiritual reality of God's work in Jesus' life, death, and resurrection. As president of the International Mission Board (IMB) of the Southern Baptist Convention from 2014–2018, David was able to advocate for the needs of orphans around the globe.[3]

While David is busily ministering and encouraging believers

to pursue the Great Commission, Heather remains just as committed to educating people on the plight of orphans around the world. "As a busy home-schooling mom of four who is trying to hold down the fort at home while my husband travels, preaches, and teaches God's Word around the world, the thought of serving orphans can feel overwhelming and distant at times," she wrote on their ministry's website, Radical. And yet the fight is too important. She suggested that people pray for God to draw families into orphan-care ministries, support families they know who are caring for orphans, and even themselves be willing to take in children. "Adoption and foster care are not for the faint of heart," Heather wrote, "but they are worth every bit of struggle, pain, joy, and excitement. I am so thankful for a sovereign God who knows what is best in each of our lives. Let's follow his commands and seek out ways to love and care for orphans."[4] Heather's exhortation reflects Jesus' statements about God's care for the disciples, for us.

## "I Will Not Leave You as Orphans"

In John 14:18, Jesus showed His heart for the vulnerable—for us. He said, "I will not leave you as orphans; I will come to you." It's important to understand that His statement is not a proof-text for orphan-care ministries. Nor is it merely an expression of His concern for the disciples as He prepares them for His departure to the Father.

Jesus was acknowledging how His disciples felt as He was explaining God's plan, which was unfolding before their very eyes. In effect, Jesus was saying, "I know what I'm saying may cause you to feel abandoned, like orphans, but do not worry!" Why?

Because Jesus' departure was the very act that would ensure they were *not* orphaned, spiritually speaking.

Orphanhood reflects the plight of lost humanity. Because of Adam and Eve's sin in the garden in Genesis 3, every human is estranged (orphaned) from God. So there is a sense of irony when Jesus told His disciples, "I will not leave you as orphans." He was talking in the context of His "farewell sermon," which took place in the Upper Room on the Thursday night before His crucifixion. Here the apostle John recorded what may be Jesus' most intimate teaching to His disciples. John began this section by showing Jesus washing the disciples' feet in John 13 and following it with His prayer for them and the church in John 17. Jesus' promise, "I will not leave you as orphans," is the second of three references related to the orphan metaphor in John 14.

Jesus began John 14 by speaking about His Father's house. This house, Jesus stated, has many dwelling places. The purpose of Jesus' departure was to go and prepare a place for the disciples to be with Him. His upcoming death, resurrection, and ascension to heaven provides all believers access to God's presence and guarantees a dwelling place with God for eternity. He told them, "Do not let your heart be troubled; believe in God, believe also in Me" (John 14:1). Why would Jesus tell His disciples not to be troubled? Because their hearts were on the verge of being troubled! Why? Because of what Jesus said in the following verses. His departure was a great threat to them. They felt, as He referenced in John 14:18, like orphans, left alone. But throughout John 14, Jesus was teaching the disciples that His death, resurrection, and ascension guaranteed that they would not be spiritual orphans. Jesus' departure ensured that His followers would be welcomed by the Father in heaven. As disciples, we have that same guarantee.

The final reference to the orphan metaphor in is John 14:23: "If anyone loves Me, he will keep My word; and My Father will love him, and We will come to him and make Our abode with him." The presence of a loving father and a dwelling place are exactly what every orphan needs and wants. Jesus assured His followers not only that they will have God as their Father but also that He and the Father will make Their home with those who love Jesus. This is the reversal of the orphan condition in the grandest scale! It is impossible for the followers of Jesus to be spiritual orphans because they themselves are the abode of their heavenly Father.

So though John 14:18 is not a proof-text for orphan-care ministries, Jesus did use this metaphor to encourage His faithful followers as they felt orphaned by His departure. But the only way for them or any human to escape spiritual orphanhood was for Him to finish His mission of death, resurrection, and ascension to heaven. That is the gospel message proclaimed in the Great Commission. Jesus' death, resurrection, and ascension enable believers to call God our heavenly Father and provide for us a forever home with God. The Great Commission was given because of humanity's orphaned condition.

## Orphan Care Near and Far

When David was pastoring in Birmingham, he decided to preach on James 1:27. Like any pastor concerned that his congregation apply the sermons he preaches, David contacted his county's agency in charge of foster children. David wanted to know if they needed foster parents. Specifically, how many families would it take to fully supply the current demands on the agency in charge of placing children in foster homes? The social worker on the other end laughed. "It would be a miracle if we had 150 more families," she told David. As David preached, he asked the congregation to pray about meeting that need and attend a meeting two weeks later if they were serious. The attendance at that meeting? One hundred and sixty families. The social worker who attended the meeting at Brook Hills inquired of David how he got so many folks to attend. David shared that what she was seeing was the work of God. "These men and women are a mirror of God's love for these kids and their families that you serve every single day."[5]

But orphan-care ministries are so difficult that at times only a few will respond to the call to foster or adopt. Ethnic and social barriers can hinder families from taking in needy kids. Through David's international ministry, he has seen how various cultures are hesitant to adopt outside their nationality: "We have been put on this earth to portray a gospel message, and that gospel message crosses physical barriers and transcends biological bloodlines."[6] This is true for every person regardless of nationality or ethnicity. While preaching in an Asian country, David shared of God's work in his and Heather's life and the joy of adoption. After the sermon, one of the church leaders approached David and told him that the concept of adoption was unfamiliar in their church. In the Asian culture, maintaining the purity of family bloodline deters families from considering adoption due to the possibility of having a mixed-race family. David's preaching plan for his ministry in that Asian church that week was changing before his eyes. For the next few days, David walked the church through biblical texts that describe adoption as gospel and family-building reality. "As I preached, it was as though I could see hearts opening across the room."[7] By the end of the conference, many in the church were signing up to learn more about how they might take in orphans—even at the expense of the cultural stigma they might have to endure.

*If God has called you to foster or adopt, He will supply you with grace necessary to go beyond your natural abilities and cultural preferences.*

Orphan-care ministries will require you to cross boundaries of some kind. Whether you sense God's call to care for vulnerable kids in your city or recognize the needs of orphans in Europe and Asia, you will likely have to overcome social, financial, and familial opposition. But know that if God has called you to foster or adopt, He will supply you with grace necessary to go beyond your natural abilities and cultural preferences. Whatever continents take up residence in your home, you will be reflecting God's heart. Let's just refuse to leave the world's children as orphans—as Jesus said.

# DISCUSSION AND REFLECTION

- How might your church help couples deal with the emotional struggles of childlessness? In what ways could your church encourage and help support foster care and adoption for these couples?
- David and Heather are parents of two adopted children and two biological children. What unique factors must be considered when parenting blended siblings?
- Read John 14:1–23. How does the concept of orphanhood characterize how the disciples felt when Jesus was preparing for His death, resurrection, and ascension?
- How does the metaphor of orphanhood characterize all people outside of Christ?
- How might orphan-care ministries advance the overall Great Commission activity of your church?

# 8

## Counterfeit Hospitality Not Welcome Here

Rosaria Butterfield is one of contemporary Christianity's leading cultural apologists. When Rosaria talks, everybody listens. Why? Because she is an insider who used to be an outsider opposed to the insiders. Her first Christian book, *The Secret Thoughts of an Unlikely Convert*, recounts Rosaria's slow, yet all-encompassing spiritual transformation from an outspoken left-wing lesbian literature professor at Syracuse University to a devout follower of Jesus. While doing research on how the "Religious Right" treated homosexuals, she published a piece criticizing the Promise Keepers movement. Readers from across the spectrum responded, but one letter in particular perplexed her.

The letter's author, a local Presbyterian pastor named Ken Smith, challenged Rosaria to think about Christianity in a different way, even asking her to give him a call so they could chat about their opposing ideas. What struck Rosaria was the author's warm and thoughtful tone. Most people who disagreed responded with hate mail. But Ken and his wife, Floy, were hospitable, inviting Rosaria to have a meal with them, at a restaurant or in their home. This was a different kind of hospitality than she was used to—eating with the enemy. Rosaria was used to what she thought was radical hospitality, sharing living space with fellow homosexuals (both male and female), welcoming to her home those suffering the effects of HIV/AIDS. But Pastor Ken Smith and his wife, Floy, were over the top.

Rosaria's curious spirit prompted her to accept the invitation. As a researcher, Rosaria was not afraid of analyzing new ideas. The Smiths fit into her broader research habits. But God was at work in Rosaria's life. Ken and Floy's genuine hospitality slowly worked its persuasive power on Rosaria's worldview and heart. The Smiths' demeanor, intellect, love for each other, and genuine interest in Rosaria shocked her. "These people simply didn't fit the stereotype and I simply didn't know what to do with this," she wrote.[1]

For the next two years, Rosaria met with the Smiths. They ate, talked, and discussed beliefs. Scripture flowed from Ken and Floy's lives into the conversations. Slowly Rosaria began to feel distant from her lesbian partner. She began to see holes in the wholeness and all-esteemed tolerance of the gay community. The next step? Attending Pastor Ken's church. Rosaria began to pray for God to reveal Himself to her, give her understanding of the gospel, and help her repent of sin. One of Pastor Ken's sermons referenced John 7:17, in which Jesus stated, "If anyone is willing to do His will, he will know of the teaching, whether it is of God or whether I speak from Myself." Rosaria knew that Christianity is a matter of submission to God from the heart, and she was ready to submit.

"Every aspect of my life came under the scrutiny of my new Christian worldview. It was like someone turned the search light on and I couldn't dim the intensity."[2] The result? A sense of relaxed, spiritual wholeness.

About a year later, Ken arranged for her a one-year teaching assignment at Geneva College, a Reformed Presbyterian school in Western Pennsylvania. Pastor Ken Smith served on the board of trustees there. While there, she asked questions about the Presbyterian denomination, Christian doctrine, and church history. She was teaching at a Bible college and getting a Bible-college education. A seminary student named Kent Butterfield helped Rosaria in her quest for answers. Within two years, Kent and Rosaria were married.

As a practicing lesbian, Rosaria had no desire for marriage. As a Christian, she embraced the idea of heterosexual, lifelong commitment. And family. When Kent and Rosaria got married, they had hoped to have children. Since Rosaria was near forty, pregnancy would be difficult without fertility treatments. The Butterfields would grow their family through foster care and adoption. They first became the foster parents of a five-month-old boy. They adopted him nine months later. Just two months after the adoption was finalized, Kent and Rosaria became the twelfth foster placement of a fifteen-year-old girl. Two years later, Kent and Rosaria adopted her. Later that year, the Butterfield household expanded again as Kent and Rosaria welcomed a newborn into their home. The Butterfields' fourth adoption was a sixteen-year-old boy.

God has taken Rosaria's heart for hospitality and applied it in the nearest sphere of her and Kent's life together, their home.

> *God has taken Rosaria's heart for hospitality and applied it in the nearest sphere of her and Kent's life together, their home.*

Rosaria also wrote a book about their experience, *The Gospel Comes with a House Key.* Rosaria wraps stories of hospitality around scriptural teaching on the subject, prodding the church to see the value of welcoming all types of people into our lives and homes for the sake of exemplifying the gospel of our hospitable God. Throughout the book, Rosaria suggests that ministries like foster care and adoption provide hospitality to some of the most vulnerable in our society.

Rosaria wrote that when she and Kent picked up their sixteen-year-old son from the group home he lived in, they felt as if they were walking off a cliff. "This is the most important endeavor, the most sacred risk, and the clearest picture of God's covenant I know of."[3] Rosaria wrote that her experience that day put left brain and right brain functions to work. The emotions fueled quantitative analysis of the situation: "Numbers go through my head when I am threatened. Now, I think about the seven thousand teenagers who 'age out' of foster care and who often end up in prison or homeless or dead. I know that this house is better than prison or homeless or dead. But still, I ponder the 105,000 children in foster care nationwide, waiting for nightmares to end."[4] As Rosaria and Kent discovered, these kids need genuine, Jesus-shaped hospitality found in homes and churches like yours.

## Counterfeit Hospitality Exposed by the Real Deal

In the Gospels, Jesus often taught in an atmosphere of controversy with the Jewish leadership. Meals with the Pharisees served as the setting for Jesus' teachings in Luke 7:36–50; 11:37–52; and 14:1–6. The latter occasion pictured what Rosaria labelled "counterfeit hospitality": "Something is counterfeit when it imitates with the intent to deceive."[5]

Luke 14 begins with a Pharisee offering fake hospitality to Jesus. He invited Jesus for the express purpose of testing Jesus regarding His activities on the Sabbath, and "they were watching Him closely" (Luke 14:1), which tips the reader that the Pharisee was indeed not a genuine host in this instance. The Pharisee and his friends scoped out Jesus to see what He would do to another notable guest, a man with dropsy. Dropsy is a disease of the kidneys and circulatory system, which causes a person to swell with fluid. The condition results in heavy breathing, general discomfort, and inability to sleep. The disease also had social implications in ancient Judaism. Many interpreted Leviticus 15:1–12 to be a basis of rendering the diseased person unclean. So why would an unclean man

> *Counterfeit hospitality is exposed by the God who comes near.*

be at the home of a Pharisee—on the Sabbath? According to New Testament scholar, Darrell Bock, in light of the Pharisees' watching eyes, "a set-up is likely."[6]

Seeing the man with dropsy, Jesus understood why the Pharisee invited Him to dine that day, at that time. He responded to the situation by asking, "Is it lawful to heal on the Sabbath, or not?" (Luke 14:3). In the midst of the Pharisees' arrogance, Jesus healed the man and sent him away. The ruse of the Pharisees was no match for Jesus' purity. Counterfeit hospitality is exposed by the God who comes near.

Jesus used this Pharisee's falsehood as a springboard for teaching about hospitality and humility. At the dinner, Jesus identified arrogance not only in the Pharisees for using the man with dropsy in their attempts to trap Him but also hubris in the guests for using their host to advance their own status. They were seeking the best seats at the meal, trying to one-up the other guests in their social circle (Luke 14:7–9). In the midst of a group concerned with cleanliness, Jesus saw filth in everyone around Him. Jesus summarized His teaching by saying, "Everyone who exalts himself will be humbled, and he who humbles himself will be exalted" (Luke 14:11).

Returning to the Pharisee hosting the Sabbath meal, Jesus challenged him that instead of hosting a meal in arrogance—like using it as a set-up by placing the needy as a testing prop—he should host meals for the purpose of bringing in outsiders. Jesus' teaching here was not just a social concern, it was rooted in His own mission as God's Son. God has come near, welcoming needy sinners to His table of forgiveness and eternal life. Should not we who have received divine benefits offer hospitality to the needy around us?

# Hospitality in the
# Home for the Long Haul

From her own experience, Rosaria knows that many foster kids are trapped in the system. Months lead to years as social workers labor to fix the damage caused by a matrix of sin, abusive parents, and poverty. "Trapped with these children," Rosaria observed, "are identities forged by trauma, neglect, self-hatred, and the degradation of drugs and poverty."[7] This sounds like the kind of person Jesus had in mind in Luke 14:12–14. Even for children who have not been severely affected by the breakdown of their family when they enter foster care or are adopted, their life as an orphan is marked by loss. Each birthday, holiday, school activity, and special event is a reminder that their life is not what it was meant to be. Even the best events have a dark cloud. Though children who are adopted enjoy the hope of a more stable future, loss still characterizes their life for years to come. "Wanted or not, adoption always starts with loss," Rosaria said. "Adoption always combines ambiguous loss with unrequested gain. An adopted child faces this paradox—this ambiguous grief—at each developmental stage."[8] Who might God call to welcome and walk through this emotional maze with children? You and your church are God's means of hospitality to vulnerable kids.

Some Christians remain hesitant to display radical hospitality to needy kids. There are just too many costs. As Rosaria noted, the fostering or adopting family must endure potential financial and relational stresses. But neither of these outweighs the potential benefits the kids and we ourselves might enjoy by welcoming needy kids into our lives. Rosaria observed that "it costs a lot of money to adopt a child through a private agency and it is 'free' to adopt a child from the public welfare system. At the same time, the moral and fiscal cost of retaining a person in the foster-care system for a lifetime is enormous. The question isn't if any of us pays for the cost of orphanhood but when—and with what kind of hope left over at the end."[9]

Some parents are concerned that practicing hospitality—like taking in orphans—might damage children already in the home. Though the relational stresses of foster care and adoption are real, the upside for the adopting Christian family should not be discounted. "Your children are learning how to live and share the gospel with fluency and how to love it before a watching world," Rosaria reminds us.[10] Indeed, "When God brings children out of neglect, abuse, dysfunction, gangs, drugs, and hate, and places them in a covenant home, he has just moved a mountain in the hearts and families of men."[11] When God moves in our hearts to open ourselves to vulnerable kids, we will better understand the way He has welcomed us into His family. Our hospitality to kids in crisis is the real deal because it reflects His hospitality to us.

◆

## DISCUSSION AND REFLECTION

- What factors in Rosaria's pre-Christian days might God have used to give her a mindset to care for orphans after she was converted? How might God use your past experiences—even as a non-Christian—to help you in your church's orphan-care ministries?
- How did Ken and Floy Smith's hospitality to Rosaria shape her view of Christianity?

- What most impacted you in Jesus' teaching on hospitality in Luke 14:1–14? How so?
- How might orphan care slip into what Rosaria calls "counterfeit hospitality"?
- In what ways can you help your church be just as concerned about hospitality to "the poor, the crippled, the lame, the blind" (Luke 14:13) as hosting family and Christian friends?

# 9

## Bedrooms, Birthday Parties, and the Gospel

Tony Merida and his wife, Kimberly, were influenced toward international adoption by watching Tony's sister's family grow through adoptions from Ethiopia. Tony and Kimberly have five children, all adopted. In 2009, Tony and Kimberly brought home a sibling set of three girls and one boy from a Ukrainian orphanage. In 2012, Tony and Kimberly became the parents of an Ethiopian boy who had been orphaned at the age of just one year old. An uncle placed him in an orphanage—one child of many, in a country and on a continent where parentless children abound. But this child was just who the Meridas wanted when they thought about expanding their family. "My Ukrainian kids interacted a lot with my sister's kids, and they really loved the Ethiopians," Tony told me. The cousin-love Tony's Ukrainian children shared with his sister's Ethiopian children contributed to Tony and Kimberly's desire to adopt again.

The gospel has compelled the Meridas along the way. "The tragedy of many orphans is that they are not only fatherless, they are also gospel-less," Tony said. "They don't have people teaching them the gospel—even in many orphanages."[1] The Meridas are fortunate that they are connected with a church that understands the importance of that ministry, as Tony is pastor for preaching and vision at Imago Dei Church in Raleigh, North Carolina. "We need to help our churches see orphan care as a part of the overall church ministry. It is not a maverick ministry," Tony said. Imago Dei carries out its vision through the P.E.A.C.E. plan: Plant churches; Evangelize the world; Aid the poor and the sick; Care for the orphan and the oppressed; Equip leaders. For Imago Dei, mercy ministries like orphan care are not divorced from the work of the Great Commission.[2]

> *"The tragedy of many orphans is that they are not only fatherless, they are also gospel-less."*

For Christians like you and me, orphan care is more than just social justice. Kids need safe homes and birthday parties. But more so, they need churches like yours where they can see the body of Christ in action and learn the gospel for themselves. That is the heart of the apostle Paul—who knew something about social justice.

## Paul, the Apostle of the Gospel to the Underprivileged

Paul's ministry travels consistently included concern for the poor. In fact, the first time a church commissioned the apostle, it was for famine relief.

The church in Antioch was founded by believers who fled Jerusalem after the stoning of Stephen (Acts 8:1–2), an event that Paul (also known as Saul), before his conversion, presided over. By Acts 11:19–22, ten years after Stephen's death, we read that the church was flourishing there. So great was its vitality that news of the Lord's blessings in Antioch reached the church leaders in Jerusalem. They in turn sent Barnabas to check on them.

What did Barnabas find in Antioch? He saw God's grace being poured on the believers, and their spiritual zeal triggered something in him. "Go get Paul!" he said to himself.

Barnabas set out for Tarsus and brought Paul to Antioch. "For an entire year they met with the church and taught considerable numbers; and the disciples were first called Christians in Antioch" (Acts 11:26).

How did this saga of Paul's early ministry in Antioch reach its zenith? Famine relief. Acts 11:27–30 records that during that fruitful season in the Antioch church, disturbing news from Jerusalem arrived. A prophet came to Antioch and predicted that a severe famine was going to come over the whole Roman world—the likes of which would prove especially challenging for minority groups like Christians. The church in Antioch responded. In a highly coordinated effort, the believers gave sacrificially and commissioned Barnabas and Paul to carry the famine relief funds to Jerusalem. The first ministry assignment Paul undertook as an official delegate of a local church was for the relief of the poor. And if Galatians 2:1–10 is a report of Paul and Barnabas's trip, their famine relief gift was well received. Indeed, in Galatians 2:10, Paul ended his account of the Jerusalem visit by noting that the elders there exhorted him "to remember the poor—the very thing I also was eager to do," Paul wrote. In *Neither Poverty nor*

*Riches,* Craig L. Blomberg wrote that "while theology and terri-
tory for ministry were still being hashed out, no debate centered
around the need to help the poor."[3]

The Jerusalem elders' exhortation to Paul in Galatians 2:10
yet rang in his ears during his second and third missionary journeys. During Paul's second journey (Acts 15:40–18:22), he traveled thousands of miles, evangelizing major cities like Philippi,
Thessalonica, Athens, Corinth, and Ephesus. Along the way, he
noticed that compared to the believers in Jerusalem and Judea,
the believers in these cities were wealthy. As Paul returned to
Jerusalem at the conclusion of his second journey, it was as if a
light bulb went off in his head: "I can go back to these churches
and inquire if they would be willing to provide financial aid for
their struggling brothers in Jerusalem and Judea!"

The transition from Paul's second journey to his third in
Acts 18:22 is so abrupt that something urgent must have been
on his mind. His letters to the Corinthians and Romans provide
windows into his rationale for this boomerang turn-around and
the launch of his third missionary journey. While staying in
Ephesus, he wrote to the Corinthian church. In 1 Corinthians
16, Paul stated one of his purposes in writing was that he hoped
to receive their collection for the needy saints in Jerusalem. Paul
urged them, "On the first day of every week each one of you is
to put aside and save, as he may prosper, so that no collections be
made when I come" (v. 2). Paul's tone in 1 Corinthians 16:1–4
has the ring of a skilled administrator—this was the apostle of
the gospel to the Gentiles laboring for the needy.

Several months after writing 1 Corinthians, Paul left Ephesus, traveling toward Corinth. Along the way he wrote 2 Corinthians and sent it ahead of him so the Corinthians would be

prepared for his arrival. Why did Paul want them to be prepared? A major theme of 2 Corinthians is this collection for the needy in Jerusalem. In 2 Corinthians 8–9, Paul picked up right where he left off at the end of 1 Corinthians. In 2 Corinthians 8:1–5, Paul noted that the churches of Macedonia—despite being less well-off than the Corinthians—had given sacrificially for the cause of famine-relief in Jerusalem. One of the purposes of Paul's third journey is now becoming clear. At each step, as Paul strengthened churches in the gospel of Christ, he also solicited funds for the needy in Jerusalem.

Romans is often considered Paul's most theologically rich letter. Here Paul detailed God's free grace to Gentiles and God's faithfulness in Christ to Israel. How did Paul conclude this message? Just before his extensive greetings in Romans 16, Paul wrote of this same famine-relief collection. Paul likely wrote Romans from Corinth (Acts 20:2–3). Imagine Paul arriving in Corinth, dealing with the spiritual struggles of the church, and then making the final administrative arrangements to get the Corinthians' large contribution back to Jerusalem. The collection fresh on his mind—and already looking to the next trip—Paul wrote Romans. He told the believers there that he would come to them after he traveled to Jerusalem "serving the saints" (Rom. 15:25). He wrote that the Corinthians (believers from Achaia) joined in contributing to "the poor among the saints in Jerusalem" (Rom. 15:26). Paul's emphasis on "the saints" being the recipients of this offering brings Paul's second and third journeys together. On his second journey, Paul recognized the wealth of the Gentile churches he visited or started and was yet aware of the impoverished Jewish believers in Jerusalem.

Paul's collection efforts on his third journey were both social justice and gospel ministry. In his commentary on Romans, Douglas J. Moo wrote, "Paul initiated this enterprise on his third missionary journey, requesting contributions from the Gentile churches he had planted to be sent to Jerusalem for the believers who were suffering from severe want."[4] Paul hoped that when the Jewish Christians in Jerusalem received the contributions he raised from among the Gentile churches, the Jerusalem church would recognize the real faith these believers had and would welcome them as brothers and sisters in Christ (Rom. 15:27–32). Though Paul's third journey was not just about this famine-relief offering, his travels cannot be understood without recognizing that for him, social justice and gospel ministry ran parallel, one stimulating the other.

Why is this important as we consider orphan care? Because while there are many subgroups of impoverished people, orphans and children in foster care are always poor. Many enter into state custody because their parents are not providing for their basic needs. Once placed in an orphanage or foster home, children remain in the same vulnerable financial state. Famine relief goes hand-in-hand with the Great Commission.

## Great Commission Orphan Care

Tony takes his responsibility of orphan care seriously, and it has affected his pastoral leadership. "One of the purposes of influence is to speak up for others who do not have someone to protect or care for them," he told me. Tony noted that while coaches, teachers, and community leaders might all be able to use their influence to care for kids in need, God has called pastors to use their influence to care for the marginalized—like orphans. "To me it's a no-brainer that we are to lead the church to care for the needy and leverage our influence for the good of those who have no influence." Tony said that if pastors wish to lead the church to care for the children of the nations or their own neighborhoods, they must do it as part of a broader pastoral ministry that follows the Scriptures as the basis of church life.

> *"Teaching the whole counsel of God, you inevitably will bump up against this idea of caring for orphans and the needy."*

"Teaching the whole counsel of God, you inevitably will bump up against this idea of caring for orphans and the needy."

But teaching and vision are only the frame for Great Commission orphan care. "We need to lead the church practically so that people are not just hearing about big concepts but are given avenues by which to pursue it," he said. "That is an important connection. We need to preach it from the stage but be able to point people to avenues and agencies through which they might carry out this vision in their specific context." In *Orphanology*, Tony wrote that in the calendar year, a pastor might lead the church to participate in an orphan Sunday or make application to orphan care around the holidays.[5] But Tony acknowledged that just as pastors talk about specific mission opportunities when they preach, they might also talk about orphan care as the context of Scripture might allow—even apart from holidays or an orphan Sunday event. "My thought on casting vision from the pulpit is to use what I call the 'drip method' of preaching," he said. "You are dripping vision week in and week out so that

God's people hear about missions, orphan care, and the like regularly through application of texts."

As we teach the gospel to children we are fostering or children we hope to adopt, we will learn more of the gospel ourselves. We will learn how much we and our churches need the gospel. In Tony's view, the brokenness of orphans helps parents and the churches they are a part of to see their own brokenness, their own inadequacies, and their dependence on God. "As a result," Tony said, "we are able to identify with orphans on a spiritual level, recognizing our own need." But this is only half of the story. "There is also a beauty in orphan care that helps us see our dignity as image bearers of God, as people who are anticipating future glory. So in many ways that brokenness and beauty characterize orphans and Christians doing orphan care."

## DISCUSSION AND REFLECTION

- What most affects you about Tony and Kimberly's adoption journey?
- Why might orphans be a "people group" that church mission teams should be especially concerned about?
- In Acts 11:27–30 and Galatians 2:10, Paul was concerned for people in poverty. How does his concern relate to his passion for the spread of the gospel?
- In Romans 15:27–32, Paul's awareness of the plight of the poor in Jerusalem shaped his ministry plans. In what ways might our churches adjust our ministry structures to better care for the poor?

- How have you seen concern for the poor and concern for evangelism work together to help your church's ministry? In what ways have you seen these hinder your church if they are out of balance?

Part 4

ORPHAN CARE AND
THE MINISTRY OF
THE LOCAL CHURCH

# 10

## Flip the Script

In the summer of 2011, Emily Johnson sensed God's call to be involved in caring for kids in the foster system. One evening, after a series of conversations about the pros and cons of foster care in which her husband, Jason, continued to share his reluctance, Emily said, "There will never be a right time to do this; there will always be a reason not to. There are kids out there who need us. The time is now."[1]

Jason had excuses—good ones. He and Emily had recently welcomed their third daughter. Plus Jason was two years into a church plant that God was blessing with substantial growth. But Jason finally agreed to Emily's prompting. On the first night of the foster-care license class, the social worker leading the class shared the story of a little girl who had just been brought into the protection of the state. The story moved Jason, who was the proud dad of three daughters. "That was it," Jason told me. "I would give my life for my daughters, and this girl had no one."

God began to show Jason that the script of excuses Jason had penned in his mind could be flipped and read as a story of potential for helping kids in crisis. He realized that being a foster parent would give Emily and him the opportunity to teach their daughters about God's generous love for them—and the need to share that love. "Perhaps my primary goal as a dad shouldn't be to raise safe girls but to raise strong ones. If our society is characterized today by anything, it's self-indulgent, self-entitled kids."[2]

He also recognized that the church he'd planted and was leading could play a significant role. "We wanted to impact the city of Houston," Jason told me. "After the first foster license class, I realized that we couldn't effectively be a church for the city and ignore this issue." God re-scripted Jason's thinking about the needs of kids in foster care and the supply of the local church. Jason knew that caring for kids in crisis is a natural outflow of the discipleship and fellowship emphases of the local church. Orphan care could be one means of following Christ and impacting Houston.

> *"Perhaps my primary goal as a dad shouldn't be to raise safe girls but to raise strong ones. If our society is characterized today by anything, it's self-indulgent, self-entitled kids."*

The growth of Jason's church from the time that he and Emily began to foster confirms that their burden for kids in crisis was not a hindrance to local church ministry. By the time the church celebrated its fourth anniversary, the staff had expanded to the point that Jason was free to pastor more and more within his niche gifting. What fueled him in those days? Equipping his church—and others—to think about the ways they could work together to impact Houston through fostering and adopting kids without a family.

God began to "flip the script," as Jason calls it, for Jason's ministry. God was refining the strategic planning and leadership giftings of a church planter to help churches see how the natural processes of discipleship and fellowship can be harnessed to help vulnerable kids.

Since then, Jason has developed curriculum to help church leaders identify various levels at which they might participate in orphan care within the broader discipleship and fellowship ministries of their churches. He now works for the Christian Alliance for Orphans, helping church leaders build systems of discipleship and support for helping kids and families in crisis.

Jason and Emily now have four daughters. They adopted the first foster child placed in their home. They have also fostered several other children, enduring the ups and downs of loving kids in crisis. Recently their circle of love has expanded beyond just children. Some of the most vulnerable kids in the foster-care system are teen moms. Twice in recent years the Johnsons have taken in teen moms in desperate need of love, structure, and support—a new script. The structure and safety of our churches and homes are not just for our structure and safety. Orphan care is a ministry full of irony: what seems like a challenge or obstacle may be an asset if we allow ourselves to view the situation through the lens of God's providence.

## What Do You Have That You Did Not Receive?

If there was a church that Paul wanted to flip the script on, it might have been the church at Corinth. The church was rich in spiritual blessings—so wealthy, that in 1 Corinthians 1, Paul's first phrases catalogued the spiritual wealth residing in these believers. He recognized that the Corinthians had been sanctified in Christ and called saints, holy ones (v. 2). He went on to recount that God had given the Corinthians grace and made them rich in all spiritual gifts (vv. 4–5). When it came to the communication arts, the Corinthian church was second to none. And Paul was confident that God would carry these believers on to the day when Christ returns, and they would be found blameless in Him (vv. 7–9).

So what needed to be flipped? With this pristine pedigree, what could be wrong? The divisions he heard had arisen in the church. Turns out, though the Corinthians were rich in spiritual blessings in Christ, they thought they needed more. They began to line up behind various human church leaders to the degree that identifying with 'x' leader and his subgroup became more prominent than identifying with the head of all churches, Christ.

Paul spent the first four chapters correcting this church's spiritual greed. Rather than rejoicing in God's grace and loving one another and the world around them, they had begun to brag about the gifting of their particular leader. "You are God's . . . building!" Paul implored them (3:9), saying that their leaders—even Apollos and Paul—were just builders. The architectural metaphor Paul applied to the Corinthians reminds us that churches in the first century gathered in households and took on the characteristics of a family. How might Paul have described the church family of Corinth? Self-centered, full of reputation and status, and empty of generous love for one another and the world. Communication arts they had; a spirit of edification and care they lacked. This makes sense. Someone climbing the ladder of status behind this leader or that one has little time for the needy around them.

How would Paul have the Corinthians flip the script? He was direct. The Corinthians needed to return to Scripture and the message of Christ, "so that no one of you will become arrogant in behalf of one against the other" (4:6). Paul wanted the Corinthians to see their richness from another angle: "What do you have that you did not receive?" he asked in 1 Corinthians 4:7. Paul's question was intended to invert the Corinthians' thinking about their affluence. Their richness was a gift from God, not a basis for bragging. And if a gift from God, a stewardship to be used.

This explains why Paul wrote the love chapter—1 Corinthians 13—as the centerpiece of chapters 12 through 14. In these three chapters Paul corrected the Corinthians' self-centered spiritual service and admonished the church to use its gifts from the foundation of love. Love is the better way to use gifts (12:31), as opposed to selfishness and bragging. Theologian Gordon D. Fee wrote that "the way they [the Corinthians] are going is basically destructive to the church as a community: the way they are being called to is one that seeks the good of others before oneself."[3] Paul wanted the Corinthians to launch their gifts from concern for those around them. Preaching, teaching, leadership, administration, and all gifts were to be employed patiently, kindly, with contentment and endurance (13:4–7).

Though out of direct context, it is not difficult to see why so many couples would want Scripture from 1 Corinthians 13 on their wedding invitations or programs. Paul described the basis of a great family! And the same can be said for a great church—one that has flipped the script from self-centeredness to

*Full of themselves and clawing for status, some churches have yet to realize that the spiritual riches they have received can only be enjoyed when given freely to those in need, like orphans.*

giving itself away as Christ did. Rosaria Butterfield's observation about greedy, stingy attitudes common in families today can be applied to contemporary churches that resemble Paul's audience in 1 Corinthians. "The household that loves things too much and loves people too little cannot honor God through the practice of radically ordinary hospitality. The household that has too much and thinks too highly of material possessions has become seduced by the idols of acquisition and achievement."[4] Full of themselves and clawing for status, some churches have yet to realize that the spiritual riches they have received can only be enjoyed when given freely to those in need, like orphans.

## Freely You Have Received, Freely Give

Many churches hesitate to launch orphan care ministries not for lack of information but because they know the cost. A church that is dedicated to helping orphans is a family prepared for soiled carpets. Some of your dishes will get broken. You will have to endure temper tantrums, lies, and runaways. Orphan care is not for churches unwilling to interrupt the schedules and existing commitments of its members. It is not for the church looking to attract only a set demographic (middle-upper class, upwardly mobile, common race). It is not for churches prioritizing their facilities' budget to keep pace with the latest decorating trends. It is not for churches that evaluate their success based on what others might think about them. As D. A. Carson wrote, "If you are constantly trying to please yourself, to make self-esteem your ultimate goal, then you are forgetting whose servant you are, whom you must strive to please."[5]

But when we willingly flip the script and freely give what we have received in Christ, orphan-care ministries become a natural extension of church life. Churches committed to discipleship and fellowship find that orphan care provides opportunities for the church to love, serve, pray, care, support, and give in tangible, relational ways. This is God's household.

## DISCUSSION AND REFLECTION

- What connections do you see between the ministries of church planting and orphan care?
- Jason was initially reluctant to foster or adopt. How might we be patient with family and friends who are hesitant to get involved in orphan care?
- How does Jason respond to those who don't want to get involved in orphan care because they are afraid it will damage their family or other children? In what ways can you respond to your friends or family when they express concern for how orphan care might hurt your family?

- Read 1 Corinthians 4 and 13. How did Paul want the Corinthians to "flip the script?"
- According to Jason, how might orphan care help a church ministry to more accurately reflect the crucifixion and resurrection of Christ?

# 11

## Trial by Fire

Bishop Aaron Blake was serving in his church and working as a counselor in the local Brownwood, Texas, school district when he became aware of the needs of kids in the foster-care system. Because these kids exhibited behavior issues and trauma, the school was reluctant to enroll them as students. "Many kids gravitated to me," Bishop Blake told me. "In the process of me seeing their anger, I began to realize that their anger was an opportunity for me to understand their trauma."

So he began to build a relationship with the administration that ran the local shelter and treatment center, which houses many kids in foster care. When those kids came to see him, he would call the shelter and get permission to take them to Dairy Queen. "I called it Blizzard therapy," he said.

When kids would have an issue, Bishop Blake would take them out for a Blizzard. In an effort to get to the core of their struggles, he would make the kids turn the Blizzard upside down and talk about why sometimes the ice cream stays in the cup and sometimes it runs out. "I would ask them about their own lives," he said. "'Why are things sometimes not coming together for you?'"

Minority teenagers in Brownwood seemed especially needy. Bishop Blake and his wife, Mary, had six grown biological children and were settling into the empty-nest phase as he began to recognize the needs of the community. So they opened their home—widely. They fostered six teenage boys, all football players at the high school where Bishop Blake served as a counselor.

That's when change really began for him. What he was experiencing at school and in his home swelled his vision for his church, Greater Faith Community Church. On November 14, 2004, burdened by the needs of kids in foster care and the local shelter, he stood before his congregation and asked if anyone would be willing to stand with him to take children into their homes, into the church.

"I had prepared a sermon to preach that morning that I had worked on all week. I stood up to bring the message when the breakfast table image of our boys came back to my mind. The faces of our sons seemed to multiply in my emotions as I recalled the image from the breakfast table earlier. I knew then that God was prompting our church to answer the call to care for children and broken families," he said.[1] He was not preaching an orphan-care sermon; he shared that his mainly African American congregation needed to understand how many of the kids in foster care are children of color. He stated that, at the time, there were about thirty thousand kids in foster care in the state of Texas. According to the most recent US census data,[2] the situation has not changed. Of the roughly four hundred thousand children in foster care, a disproportionately high number are minority.

Bishop Blake encouraged his congregation to get involved.

The response that day was overwhelming. Person after person stood, accepting the invitation. "Then I preached one of the worst messages I have ever preached because I was so over-whelmed with what we might be able to do," he said. He asked the folks who stood to remain after the service, and he shared further about what he believed God was calling the church to do: they would invite the county child placement agency to set up an office in their church and begin classes for the Greater Faith members who wanted to foster or adopt. The county officials would help church members with the background checks, CPR certification, and the necessary paperwork, while Bishop Blake would lead spiritual development for the parents and families taking in these children.

Everyone agreed, and within three months, thirty-nine children were placed in church families. The church had less than two hundred in Sunday attendance at the time. For the next twelve years, Greater Faith averaged fifty-five child placements per year. "We chased the data," Bishop Blake said. "We knew that kids needed to stay in their school, in their community, and our church could be the link." The church made it a goal to flip the supply-demand balance, to have more families waiting for kids than kids waiting for families, and they did.[3] The second Sunday of November, in conjunction with the day that he asked his church to get involved with the needs of vulnerable kids in their community, has become a holiday of sorts in the orphan-care movement. The Global Orphan Project annually promotes "Stand Sunday,"[4] during which pastors might likewise call their churches to become involved in orphan care.

County administrators took note of Bishop Blake's leader-ship and the work of Greater Faith Community Church. They inquired if he would help them replicate Greater Faith's ministry in other churches and communities. What began in Brownwood, Texas, has spread across the nation through the ministry of Care Portal, an extension of the Global Orphan Project.[5] Care Portal connects social workers and specific families in need with churches willing to help, often preventing children from being removed from their current home.

## The Normal, Supernaturally United Church

On November 14, 2004, many families and individuals of Greater Faith Community Church stood in commitment to foster or adopt. God compelled a large proportion of the church to get involved and to do so immediately. The quantity of believers who stood that day created momentum for each participant. They understood that together they could make an impact, that together they could help one another through the processes of licensure, certification, placement, and transition. It is often said that strength comes in numbers, and this maxim has proven true at Greater Faith Community Church. I am not suggesting that we should all expect to see God replicate His work in our churches as He has done through Greater Faith. But I fear that we who are concerned for our churches and the

> *I fear that we who are concerned for our churches and the needs of orphans often expect too little of God and each other. This is unbiblical.*

needs of orphans often expect too little of God and each other. This is unbiblical.

In Acts 2, Luke described the descent of the Spirit at Pentecost and the founding of the church in Jerusalem. He noted that from its conception, the local church has been a supernaturally unified and living organization. The believers "were continually devoting themselves to the apostles' teaching and to fellowship, to the breaking of bread and to prayer" (Acts 2:42). Luke even provided specifics on how the members of the church cared for one another: these believers "were together and had all things in common" (v. 44). What a remarkable scene! But this is not all. In the next verse, Luke wrote about the degree to which the believers in Jerusalem displayed mutual concern for one another: "They began selling their property and possessions and were sharing them with all, as anyone might have need." The Jerusalem church was willing to go to extremes—and since everyone was ready to participate, the extreme acts seemed normal. This common sacrifice for common cause defines the idea of church fellowship in the New Testament.

As believers come together in partnership, God works through us to stimulate and encourage each other in His work. If the initial scene of church fellowship in the New Testament records such acts of sacrifice as selling property and giving proceeds for common needs, would it be too much of us to expect God to bring people in our churches together for great causes like orphan care? While walking the foster or adoption journey with a group from your church might require financial sacrifice, it more likely would require time, prayer, encouragement, presence, and a listening ear. In short, the kind of commitment we would have to display together would not be new for a New

Testament church. As you join with other families and church
leaders to foster, adopt, or support those who do, you provide
a beam of strength through which God will glorify Himself in
your church.

## Engrafted

When Bishop Blake approached his church that Sunday in November, his congregation already knew he was committed to the
kids he and Mary were fostering. Earlier that year, the boys had
accidently set the Blake house on fire. At 3 a.m. in early January,
one of the boys ran into the Bishop Blake and Mary's bedroom
screaming, "Pop, my room is on fire!" Flames were already in the
attic when Bishop Blake ran into the room. He tried to put out
the fire but was unsuccessful, so he gathered the family and fled.
They stood in the front of their home—the home where he and
Mary had raised their six biological children—and watched it
burn to the ground.

"I was thinking about all the memories, all the Christmases,
all the pictures that were going up in flames," he told me. That
moment represented a decisive shift. The burning house represented his memories of raising his six children. The six foster
sons standing beside him represented his future parenting
responsibilities.

What to do next? Go to Walmart. Bishop Blake loaded up
the family and headed to Walmart to buy clothes and necessities
for school, where the boys would be the next day. Having made
their purchases, they headed to a hotel to get a few hours of
sleep before beginning a new day. But the boys resisted going
to school. Bishop Blake couldn't understand why they refused.

Was it the Walmart attire? Embarrassment about the fire? He knew that if the boys were not at school, they could not go to football practice. Missing practice might jeopardize playing in that Friday's game. Why would the boys forfeit the opportunity to play in a game they had looked forward to?

The truth finally came out. The boys had enough collective experience to know the routine: you mess up like this at a foster home, and you are gone.[6] They expected social services employees to greet them after school, not the Blakes. That morning Bishop Blake presided as judge and parent in an informal adoption ceremony.

"You are no longer a foster kid," he told them. "You will always be a Blake. You have been engrafted." So powerful was that event that one of their adopted sons, Christian rapper Diego Fuller, produced an album titled *Engrafted*,[7] which contains these lyrics:

> I got Christ that's within
> He took the old me, and burned him up
> So, I been grafted in.

What a beautiful gift Christ gives us. What a beautiful gift we can present on Christ's behalf to orphans!

## DISCUSSION AND REFLECTION

- Has your pastor ever given a call to action to your church? What was it for? What were the results?
- God's work through Bishop Blake's church is remarkable. How might we encourage believers in churches where they are one of only a handful of families concerned for orphans?
- How might your church partner with a local school or school district to care for kids in foster care or shelters?
- Read Acts 2:41–47. Why was the church's unity emphasized here?
- How can you unite with those in your church and your church leaders to further partner in orphan care?

# 12

◆

# Might a Social Worker Be Your Next Church Hire?

Bob Miller has been the pastor of Wellspring Community Church in St. Joseph, Missouri, since it began in 2006. In Wellspring's early days, they hosted lots of events for the community. "We did great Easter egg hunts!" Bob told me. "But we would just parachute into the neighborhood for an event and then leave. We never really developed lasting relationships." Looking for a new strategy, Bob's church began to serve the local school district, such as by painting an elementary school's teachers' lounge. "The principal of that school has not stopped coming to our church since that service project," Bob said.

In time they became more involved with the kids—mentoring, tutoring, or playing with them. But Wellspring's influence in the neighborhood was initiated by a member of their congregation who had a heart for kids and a love of basketball. He noticed that the kids at the school did not have a basketball team and discovered that none of the parents had enough margin in their lives to coach a kids' team. So with the help of his small group, this man decided to start a fifth-grade basketball program there." The small group paid the fees for the kids to enter a league, purchased their equipment, and shuttled them to games. Over the next three years, the program exploded and the church was coaching five different teams. "All of a sudden, you've got relationships with fifty or so kids and some parents as well," Bob said.

It was evident to Wellspring's leaders that God was beginning to work not only through their church but also through others in the neighborhood. And they tapped in to what He was doing by developing partnerships. "During one summer, we came across this couple that made sandwiches for 150 neighborhood kids every day," he told me. "They were literally driving up and down the neighborhood streets giving out food." This couple's church was not able to help with financial support, so a local food bank and generous restaurants provided donations. "There was no plan—at all!" Wellspring helped this couple to establish a 501(c)(3) for financial gifts and accountability and began to help with the sandwiches too.

As members of Wellspring were shuttling kids to games and helping make sandwiches, they would often enter the homes of these children, getting an up-close view of their living conditions and circumstances. That's when the man who created the basketball program created another ministry: "a safe house in the neighborhood where kids could have a formative Christian environment," Bob explained. Many of the kids had such difficult living situations that they were on the borderline of being placed in foster care. The Wellspring house would serve as a stabilizing resource in the midst of challenging family conditions. In 2014, this vision came to fruition. Wellspring purchased and renovated a home in the neighborhood, turning it into a privately run, temporary housing facility. They call it the Guest House.

During those years when Wellspring was working to mentor elementary school kids through basketball, the Lord saved a young social worker who served in a St. Joseph boys' home. "When she heard we were thinking about buying a home and having a ministry base in the community, she said, 'I'll do it!'" Bob told me. "She had become frustrated with being in a secular work environment and not being able to share the love of Christ with the kids she was ministering to. So essentially we were hiring a missionary."

Ministry compels ministry. "Once we purchased the Guest House, we had an immediate opportunity for the whole church to step in." Orphan-care ministries in a local church compel believers with various giftings to step up and serve, sometimes even stimulating church leaders to new avenues of ministry.

Despite all God was doing in and through Wellspring, Bob resisted God's call to adopt. He and his wife, Kristen, had three biological children and ministry opportunities all around them. But they also had one open seat at their dining room table. "God would not let me off the hook. If I was going to continue to lead the church in this direction, I would need to step in more personally," Bob said. So compelling was the mutual service and stimulation of God's work in the church that Bob—the founding pastor—was compelled to further invest. This is ministry coming full circle. In 2013, after five years in foster care ministry, Bob and Kristen adopted internationally from Ethiopia.

## The Church Being the
## Church for the Next Generation

God's work through Wellspring and Bob is a testimony to the fact
that when the local church gathers, God stirs up the gifts of His
people. One believer shares a vision with another believer, creating a sense of momentum for ministry. This is what the author
of Hebrews had in mind when he exhorted his readers—a local assembly of believers he knew personally—to prioritize their
regular gatherings. In Hebrews 10:25, he encouraged them to
continue meeting regularly despite the fact that some Christians
had slacked in their commitment to come together. This verse is
rightly spoken by church leaders as a reminder that busy believers
under their care should make church attendance a staple in their
family schedule. But the author of Hebrews wrote this verse as an
expression of carrying out his exhortation in the previous verses,
in which he declared that the church must labor to maintain its
confession of Christ and "consider how to stimulate one another
to love and good deeds" (10:24).

The author of Hebrews was not concerned just with believers gathering together, but with what happens when believers
gather. His motive was that the church maintain a structure
by which it might build itself vertically *and* horizontally. In his
mind, church meetings were not ends in themselves.

Attendance matters only for the sake of what the attendees
do at and as a result of their gatherings. When the church as-
sembles, it is to remember God's blessings in Christ and the
gifts and opportunities God has set upon the members of the
church. "There is amazing power in an encouraging word," wrote
R. Kent Hughes in *Hebrews: An Anchor for the Soul.* "You and I

can change a life with a kind word. Encouragement is a Christian duty. Lives of provocation through prayer, example, Scripture, and encouragement are gifts the church needs desperately."[1] And when those gifts are a regular part of church life? Those believers represent Christ in the world. Can you see how Wellspring's decision to purchase the Guest House and staff it as an expression of faith would compel the author of Hebrews to say, "Amen!"?

This exhortation to community edification in Hebrews 10:23–25 is in fact the third time in the letter that he calls the church to a lifestyle of mutual edification. In Hebrews 3:12–14, the author encouraged the church to look around and be aware of the needs of their brothers and sisters in Christ. The author's specific concern was for the members of the congregation to help them persevere in Christ, together fighting the temptation to turn away. Apostasy is a real danger—and the author of Hebrews proposed that believers in a mutually concerned congregation become God's means of grace for perseverance.

One facet of perseverance is service. As we use our gifts, supported by our brothers and sisters in Christ, we grow closer to Christ and continue in the faith. And those whom we support grow in their faith as they serve. As theologian F. F. Bruce wrote, "In a fellowship which exercised a watchful and unremitting care for its members the temptation to prefer the easy course to the right one would be greatly weakened, and the united resolution to stand firm would be correspondingly strengthened."[2] Those serving in orphan care need the kind of mutuality that Hebrews sets as a lifestyle for all Christians.

"Those participating in orphan care enter full-in," Bob told me. "And many in the church are called to wrap-around care for the families who take in kids." Wellspring has experienced what Russell Moore observed when he wrote, "Adoption can be a priority for everyone within the church in ways that reflect the diversity and unity of a church that is one body with many members. Adoption can be part of our congregational lives."[3]

The author of Hebrews is known for warning believers in danger of lapsing or falling from faith. He stated that good works done in love are the mark of endurance. Following an extended warning in Hebrews 6:1–8, the author was nonetheless confident of his audience. Why? "For God is not unjust so as to forget your work and the love which you have shown toward His name, in having ministered and in still ministering to the saints" (v. 10). Foster care and adoption are organic ministries for a church committed to serving its members in love. These ministries can even stimulate the local church to greater service.

*It is not* **whether** *you are going* *to be engaged, but* **how.**

## The Broken Are the Best Healers

"We have no choice about the families we are born into," Bob told me. "But we can do something about the broken family situations that the next generation is currently enduring." Wellspring's heartbeat is to create a new normal for the next generation—and that is Bob's life mission too. Before Bob was fifteen, he had watched three divorces take place in the lives of his parents. In addition, Bob was physically and verbally abused. Bob understood what trauma looks and feels like, so it made sense to him that God would give Bob a heart for kids and lead him into education, missions, local church ministry, and orphan care ministry.

Hiring a social worker to live at the Guest House connected the church to the local division of the Department of Children and Family Services (DCFS). Wellspring soon learned of the need for local foster parents. "When I found out that there is an average of seventy-five to eighty kids in foster care in my county and only ten licensed foster families in a city of one hundred thousand people, that gets my attention," Bob said. In January 2017, Bob took those numbers to his church and set a goal of five families who would enroll in foster-care training and another ten who would offer wrap-around support for the five foster families. "In the first three or four months, twelve families stepped up to foster or adopt," Bob said. "In our church, it is not *whether* you are going to be engaged, but *how*. I don't leave a lot of wiggle room for folks, because this is who we are."

Bob's reflection reminds me of Mez McConnell and Mike McKinley's exhortation to church leaders when they wrote in *Church in Hard Places*, "Starbucks sells coffee, Listerine makes mouthwash, and the church holds out the gospel and trains people to obey by doing the work of ministry. If we don't do it, no one will. If we do anything else, we are getting off track."[4] Foster-care and adoption ministries provide the local church opportunities to partner together in tangible gospel work. To many, orphan care is often thought to be a burden on the church, but as we foster or adopt, we are both doing good for vulnerable kids and doing good for our churches by providing pathways of ministry for our brothers and sisters to use the gifts God has given them.

# DISCUSSION AND REFLECTION

- Early in Wellspring's ministry, Bob saw that his church was not developing deep relationships with the community they were trying to reach. Why is relational depth necessary for gospel ministry?
- What is your church's relationship with the school districts surrounding your meeting places? How might your church more deeply love the people of your community by being involved in the schools?
- Read Hebrews 3 and 10:19–25. What do these passages teach about the way Christians should relate with one another?
- How does a church's concern for healthy, mutually edifying relationships provide a foundation for orphan-care ministries?
- For several years, Bob resisted God's call to adopt. Have you ever hesitated to embrace God's call to a specific ministry? What was the result? How might you help fellow believers submit to God's call in a particular way?

# Part 5

◆

# ORPHAN CARE AND
# RACE RELATIONS

# 13

◆

# No Race Left Out

John Mark and Angie Yeats were raised in Christian homes. Both had parents active in vocational ministry and instilled in John Mark and Angie a vision for the power of the gospel. Aware of the needs of children without parents, the Yeatses thought they would initiate foster care or even an adoption after having biological children. But God had other plans.

The Yeatses discovered that they would not be able to conceive children biologically. So John Mark and Angie educated themselves on the process of adoption. One agency provided the Yeatses with a worksheet to help them identify the characteristics of children they would or would not be open to having in their home. If John Mark and Angie were not able to handle children with special needs, medical challenges, or severe emotional problems, the agency wanted to know up front. One of the categories on the worksheet concerned race. Would the potential parent(s) decline a child of 'x' race?

God used that worksheet to establish a strategic plan for the Yeatses—a framework that would influence their extended family and the churches and seminaries John Mark would help lead in the years to come. The Yeatses made a faith commitment that if they received a child of a minority race, they would seek to adopt another child of that same race. This decision would ensure that if one of their children was of a minority race, that child would not be the only member of their immediate family of that particular racial background.

When John Mark and Angie learned they could welcome a four-month-old African American girl into their family, they responded, "Blessed be the name of the Lord!" In time, the Lord gave the Yeatses one other girl and two boys. White parents with four black children. Given that my family is also racially diverse, I enjoy a special fellowship with John Mark. When my two African American girls moved in, John Mark was one of the first people I contacted, and we got our kids together to have hot chocolate at a local Barnes & Noble. Two white men, four African American girls, one deck of UNO cards.

The Yeatses knew that when they committed to making sure no child in their immediate family would be racially isolated, they themselves might eventually be the minority race in their own home. Having roots in the American South, the Yeatses knew that their extended network might not share their enthusiasm at becoming parents of African American children. But John Mark and Angie's concerns were put to rest as extended family embraced and celebrated their growing family—despite racial differences.

The racial diversity of John Mark and Angie's family also influenced their ministries. They understood that as parents of four African American children, they would need to seek out racially diverse neighborhoods to live in, racially diverse school settings for their children's education, and churches that embraced racial diversity.

"It is a front-line issue," John Mark told me. "I think it is a front-line issue for the gospel—and if my church doesn't want to hear that, they are not going to put up with us for very long." Yet by God's grace, their family's racial diversity has actually torn down walls. John Mark noted that the churches he has served have become increasingly multiethnic because of the makeup of his family and the conversations he has been able to initiate concerning racial issues. Their family's racial diversity has helped them counsel many believers in the churches they have served, as well as students at seminaries where John Mark has taught.

But a theme of that counsel is that racial hostility still exists in the culture. As a Christian leader, John Mark cannot but be compelled to address these racial issues—especially when his children are bullied and told that their place is back in Africa, that they might be next on the list to be lynched, that they cannot keep their hair in a natural fashion because it would violate school policy. "You begin to realize the pervasive biases that are in our culture against our brothers and sisters," John Mark told me. "And that is not okay."

## With One Voice, Glorify God

It was not okay for the apostle Paul either. When folks begin to read the New Testament seriously for the first time, they are often struck by how practical it is. The teachings of authors like Paul transcend cultural specifics and take root even in the modern world. Just beneath the New Testament's surface, one discovers that racial tensions between Jews—the physical descendants of

Abraham—and Gentiles—all other races, sometimes referred to as "Greeks"—permeated life in the first century.

Paul knew this racial tension as well as anyone. The book of Acts describes Paul as a Jew zealous for the traditions of his nation. He believed that devotion to the Old Testament laws for Jews to separate themselves from Gentiles was second to none for spirituality. That is why he could approve the stoning of Stephen (Acts 8:1), who had challenged Jewish beliefs about God's dwelling in the Jews' temple in Jerusalem (7:44–50). But Paul's way of thinking changed when the Lord appeared to him. Romans is Paul's most complete, systematic letter—and in it he portrays racial unity as a theological issue. For Paul, the gospel of Christ is so powerful that it can foster a desire for racial unity even among the most divided races. Indeed, racial unity is a theme we can trace from Romans 1 to Romans 15.

In Romans 1:14, Paul made what for many Jews would have been a shocking and even blasphemous statement: he said he was obligated to Gentiles! How could a Jew of pure national descent like Paul be obligated to outsiders like Gentiles and barbarians? Because of the gospel, Paul wrote in the next verse. Paul had come to understand that all people need the same message of salvation: "For I am not ashamed of the gospel, because it is God's power for salvation to everyone who believes, first to the Jew, and also to the Greek. For in it God's righteousness is revealed from faith to faith, just as it is written: The righteous will live by faith" (Rom. 1:16–17 HCSB). Paul described the gospel as potent among all people groups, broadening the scope of God's blessing on Israel. Author Douglas J. Moo commented, "Announcing what will become a key note in this letter, Paul insists that the salvation available in the gospel is for *all* who believe (3:22; 4:11, 16; 10:4,

11–13; cf. 11:32; 16:26). In a significant advance on the Old Testament, which focused on Israel, the gospel is universally available."[1] This universally available gospel establishes the framework for racially diverse churches. Because of the racial diversity of kids in foster care and orphanages around the globe, churches

> *Because of the racial diversity of kids in foster care and orphanages around the globe, churches have the opportunity to appreciate how the gospel unifies diverse races.*

that participate in foster care or adoption have the opportunity to appreciate how the gospel unifies diverse races. The gospel unifies different races because we all equally need God's grace.

In Romans 1:18–3:26, Paul explained why all people need the good news of salvation by faith in Christ. Because both Jews and Gentiles are guilty—really guilty!—before God. So bad is the human situation that even the racial heritage of the Jewish nation is of little consequence before God's righteous standards. In the middle of Romans 3, Paul assembled several Old Testament texts to make his point. He began his list of quotes by citing Psalms 14 and 53, writing, "There is no one righteous, not even one" (Rom. 3:10 HCSB). At its core, racism is an expression of human pride. And Romans 1:18–3:26 highlights the foolishness of human pride, removing the foundation of racial tensions between Jews and Gentiles in the ancient world and the basis of racially motivated pride in our day as well. Many churches know this in an academic sense. Foster care and adoption help us appreciate it personally.

Paul's dismal portrait of humanity provides the backdrop for the beauty of the gospel. This is the drama of Scripture! In a heightened pitch we read, "But now apart from the Law the righteousness of God has been manifested, being witnessed by the Law and the Prophets, even the righteousness of God through faith in Jesus Christ for all those who believe; for there is no distinction" (Rom. 3:21–22). Paul's statement, "there is no distinction," places all races in the same position. All need to be accepted by God through faith in Christ and not their moral status or racial heritage. For Jews like Paul, who had once leaned their relationship with God upon the supposed bulwark of their racial heritage, God's grace toward Gentiles seemed anything but righteous. That is why Romans 11:33–36 (ESV) concludes with a doxology fueled by questions:

> Oh, the depth of the riches and wisdom and knowledge of God! How unsearchable are his judgments and how inscrutable his ways!
>
> "For who has known the mind of the Lord,
>     or who has been his counselor?"
> "Or who has given a gift to him
>     that he might be repaid?"
>
> For from him and through him and to him are all things. To him be glory forever. Amen.

Paul's string of quotations from Isaiah 40:13, Job 41:11, and Jeremiah 23:18 in this passage are all answered with a resounding, "No one!" God had indeed enacted a surprising, racially impartial message in Christ. At the front door of every local church thus hangs a sign reading, "HUMILITY REQUIRED." And churches that participate in foster care and adoption come to appreciate how racial diversity reinforces gospel humility. When kids from another race become a part of the church family, prejudices are exposed, sin is revealed, and God's grace in the gospel takes center stage. God's righteousness, His fairness, is the only foundation on which anyone in the church can stand.

What is Paul's intention in describing the sin of both Jews and Gentiles before God's impartial judgment? As the Jews and Gentiles in Rome came to understand their common needy position before God, their divisive arsenal of pride would crumble. Humility is the foundation of unity. Paul's choice of words in Romans 12:1 demonstrates his motive: "Therefore I urge you, brethren, by the mercies of God, to present your bodies a living and holy sacrifice, acceptable to God, which is your spiritual service of worship." Did you catch the numerical nuance of the verse? Paul urged Jews and Gentiles—because they have both received the common mercies of God—to offer their bodies (plural) as a (singular) sacrifice to God. Paul imagined both groups climbing on the sacrificial altar together as a unified offering of praise to God!

The patterns of life in Paul's world were built on principles of hierarchy and racism. But he contradicted it by telling his readers, "Do not be conformed to this world" (Rom. 12:2). And as J. Daniel Hays wrote in *From Every People and Nation*, "The cross of Christ demolished all barriers between people and God, reconciling people who believe, both to God and to each other. This horizontal reconciliation applies in particular to those Christians who differ from each other and between whom there exists traditional culture-driven hostility."[2]

## New Sets of Lenses

Racial tensions are among the most pressing culturally driven hostilities of our day. For John Mark and Angie Yeats—like many Christians—concerns for racial reconciliation are rooted in the New Testament. "When you enter into the conversation with new sets of lenses, you ask different questions," John Mark told me. "If a church leader has a past marked by drug or alcohol issues, he will likely emphasize God's power over those challenges. The same with racial issues. Parents of minority children will likewise be sensitive to racial issues." That's why understanding Paul's ideas in Romans is so beneficial for churches doing the work of orphan care. Paul's plan for humbling and unifying the mixed Jew/Gentile churches in Rome reaches its zenith in Romans 15, in which he urged these diverse races to go beyond just putting up with one another. He told them to please one another! Paul envisioned a diverse congregation where various ethnic backgrounds see themselves as at the service of other races, even their historical enemies! What led Paul to write such a radical statement? The fact that even Christ did not live to please Himself (v. 3). Indeed, though Jews and Gentiles had a storied history, they were to accept one another just as Christ accepted them, to God's glory (v. 7). That command, according to theologian Jarvis J. Williams, was "a call to Jews and Gentiles to accept one another since Paul gives this command in a context in which he speaks of Jesus becoming a servant for Jews and Gentiles."[3] Since Jews and Gentiles were equally

*The gospel is the answer for racial pride and division surfacing in any culture.*

guilty before God, they had no basis for one-upmanship. Paul's prayer was that God would grant them to be of a united mind "so that with one accord you may with one voice glorify the God and Father of our Lord Jesus Christ" (v. 6).

The gospel is the answer for racial pride and division surfacing in any culture. Sadly, because the church has historically not been known for racial unity, the culture does not look first to the church for solutions to the racial strife of our day. But Paul's thesis in Romans is as potent for modern America as it was for ancient Rome. As it is the case that a disproportionate number of orphans are of minority races, churches concerned for orphans will have the opportunity to demonstrate Paul's message of God's righteousness to all peoples. You too may see the gospel—and skin color—through a new set of lenses.

# DISCUSSION AND REFLECTION

- What factors might you have to consider if you were to foster or adopt a child of a different race?
- John Mark Yeats stated that parenting African American children has increased his sensitivity to racial tensions. What might you do to see racial issues through the lenses of a different race?
- Have you known foster or adoptive families who faced opposition from their own extended family because they took in a child of a different race? How did the foster or adoptive parents respond?
- How might your church help a family who is hesitant to take in a child of a different race?
- Read Romans 3 and 15:1–13. What does Paul state is the basis of gospel unity for all races?

# 14

---

# Transracial Adoption
# Comes to Television

John and Terri Moore remember September 11, 2001, as a tragic day in American history. But the terrorist attacks on the East Coast provided a life-changing blessing for the Moores in Long Beach, California. The magnitude of that morning's events quickly rippled across the US time zones, and the Los Angeles County Courthouse, like many civic buildings, closed without notice.

The Los Angeles County Court docket for September 11, 2001, included a hearing that would have, based on the court's interpretation of the Indian Child Welfare Act (ICWA), removed two children from John and Terri's custody—children whom they had hoped to adopt.[1] The boys were four and five years old when John and Terri got them in July 2000. At that time, the Moores were designated as foster parents. But since no relatives stepped up to take the children, Los Angeles County Social Services placed the boys on a "fast-track" adoption with John and Terri.

All was well until December 2000, when John and Terri learned that their future sons were one-sixteenth Native American. The foster-care system's core values include the notion that biological children should be kept with biological family members as often as possible, if this can be done safely. The ICWA reflects that principle and was passed in order to preserve Native American culture. The delay of court proceedings in Los Angeles County allowed John and Terri to learn a great deal about the ICWA, even to the point that they were educating some of the attorneys and Los Angeles County Social Services. It also allowed county officials to dig further into the case and look at the children's best interests with fresh eyes. John and Terri's experience has led them to advocate for the repeal of the ICWA, and John even had the opportunity to share their story as part of a feature on the ICWA for the popular *Dr. Phil* television show in 2012.[2]

In time, the judge presiding over John and Terri's case decided it was in the boys' best interest that they be placed permanently with the Moores. In April 2003, the boys' adoption was finalized. Though John and Terri could have biological children, they have chosen to be a family for several kids in foster care and expand their family through adoption. They are adoptive parents of seven children representing five races: Native American, Hispanic, Cambodian, Caucasian, and African American. When they adopted each child, the Moores lived in Long Beach. Their family reflected the racial diversity of the city—but not their church at that time.

Despite ministering in such a racially diverse area, their church was Caucasian. As the Moore family grew in quantity and diversity, however, John and Terri's friends at church began to inquire about how they too might get involved in foster care and adoption. "It became a movement," John told me. "It helped our church look outward. Fostering was not the only outlet for the macro theme of outreach and love for neighbor that we heard preached on Sundays, it became a suitable outlet for many." Over the next few years, "Our Sunday school classes resembled the United Nations," John said. At one point, about 20 percent of the kids enrolled in Sunday school were in foster care or had been adopted.

As their church increased in racial diversity, it continued to maintain a loving attitude that prevented racial strife from causing division. But when the Moores moved to Virginia, their African American daughter became the subject of racial bullying. Unfortunately, John has seen that black children have it worse than children of other races. John has had to counsel his daughter and discuss with school officials what policies are in place for kids who might be bullied because of their race.

Adopting a racially diverse family has also opened his eyes to a better understanding of the gospel. "It has helped me to see that the gospel I grew up with was very small," he told me. "Before getting involved in foster care, I thought the gospel was concerned with my own personal salvation, and that is it. But God is concerned to renew all of creation. In the new creation, no child will be without a family, and we should let our families point to the new creation family portrait." What a powerful reminder for the church. As we partner together in our local churches to foster or adopt, our eyes will be opened to the needs of kids and the resources that we have together in the gospel. As we help kids, we help ourselves understand God's eternal plan for all nations.

# Building One
# New Humanity in Christ

In Ephesians, Paul painted a portrait of God's eternal plan to unify all nations in Christ. Paul's prayer at the end of Ephesians 3 is one of his most beloved intercessions. He asked God to establish the church in love that they would know "the breadth and length and height and depth" of God's love for them (v. 18). Paul's language here reflects the Old Testament descriptions of Solomon's temple as recorded in 1 Kings 6:2–3, "As for the house which King Solomon built for the LORD, its length was sixty cubits and its width twenty cubits and its height thirty cubits. The porch in front of the nave of the house was twenty cubits in length, corresponding to the width of the house, and its depth along the front of the house was ten cubits." Why would Paul employ construction imagery to describe the Ephesians' relationship with God—imagery that would call to mind Solomon's temple?

Paul's prayer in Ephesians 3:14–19 culminates references to a building metaphor he employed throughout the first three chapters of Ephesians. Here Paul told the story of God's work of building for Himself a mammoth temple composed of all races of humanity with Christ Himself as the capstone. In Ephesians 1:10, Paul wrote that God's purpose in the revelation of the gospel is to sum up all things in Christ, things in heaven and things on earth in Him. Paul's reference to "things" involves two ideas—ages of history and races of humanity. In a perfectly balanced sequence, Paul first described Jews like himself who hoped in Christ (Eph. 1:11–12) and then those of the Gentiles—like the Ephesians—who also heard the message of Christ and received the Holy Spirit (vv. 12–14).

Paul wrote that God raised up Christ and "seated Him at His right hand in the heavenly places, far above all rule and authority and power and dominion, and every name that is named, not only in this age but also in the one to come" (Eph. 1:20–21). For Paul, Christ's resurrection is evidence of His supremacy; the One in whom all things are summed up (Eph. 1:10) is the One who rules over all spiritual powers. He is the capstone of God's temple that stretches even to the heavens. And this temple is made up of all races. John Moore's Sunday school class was a miniature display of what God is building for eternity.

In Ephesians 1, Paul used a construction metaphor to express theology, and in Ephesians 2 he used that same imagery to describe all races built together in Christ, stating that believers are God's workmanship created in Christ Jesus for good works (2:10). Paul's "we" in Ephesians 2:10 refers to both Jews and Gentiles, all races of humanity. Through the remainder of Ephesians 2, Paul detailed how God has built this transnational temple in Christ. Though historically Jews separated themselves from Gentiles and Gentiles were thought strangers to the promises God made to Israel (vv. 11–12), when Christ came, their status changed. As Greg Beale suggested in *The Temple and the Church's Mission*, "Why does Paul mention that Gentiles formerly were separated from Israel's 'promise' (v. 12) but 'now' are fellow-sharers in that 'promise' (3:6)? The reason, in part, is to underscore that Gentiles are identified in Ephesians 2:19–22 with the long-awaited temple promised in Isaiah and the other prophets."[3]

Through Christ's blood, God has brought Gentiles near as well (Eph. 2:13). In His death and resurrection, Christ has broken down the dividing wall of the Old Testament law. The result? God has created "one new man" (Eph. 2:15) out of the historically divergent Jew/Gentile races. Historical enemies made brothers and sisters. "Here's where, I think, the nub of the whole issue lies," wrote Russell Moore in *Adopted for Life*. "Adoption would become a priority in our churches if our churches themselves saw our brotherhood and sisterhood in the church itself rather than in our fleshly identities."[4]

> *This is the drama of Scripture! God has constructed a new entity, a new corporate body made of all nationalities.*

This is the drama of Scripture! God has constructed a new entity, a new corporate body made of all nationalities. And churches that participate in orphan care have the opportunity to appreciate the massive, multiethnic temple God is building. As Jarvis J. Williams wrote in *One New Man*, "No ethnic boundary marker or cultural idiosyncrasy matters anymore since Jesus' death ends the hostility between Jews and Gentiles who believe, and then makes both groups into one new man."[5] All peoples come to God only through Christ, "having been built on the foundation of the apostles and prophets, Christ Jesus Himself being the corner stone, in whom the whole building, being fitted together, is growing into a holy temple in the Lord, in whom you also are being built together into a dwelling of God in the Spirit" (Eph. 2:20–22).

Paul's use of a construction metaphor would have spoken to his audience. Acts 19 records that the temple of Artemis—one of the greatest structures of the ancient world—was located in Ephesus. He used that metaphor to show that God is creating for Himself a new kind of temple, one made of people who were once characterized by racial enmity but through His work in Christ are now characterized by peace.

One unique feature of Paul's construction metaphor is that he pictured a temple that is alive. So animate is this new temple that in Ephesians 4 Paul described it as a body that builds itself in love. Though this temple-body is characterized by racial diversity, it is also to be characterized by truthful, loving speech, growing up in every way into Christ, the head (v. 15). As each member makes his or her contribution, this new, living temple-body builds itself up in love (v. 16).

## Arms Wide to a Needy World

We are called to contribute to building the church through all peoples, something John and Terri Moore take seriously. Before serving in various capacities to help equip Christians and churches to take in orphans, John was a screenwriter and worked in production in Hollywood. Now John helps rewrite the stories of orphaned children. He speaks around the United States at events like Focus on the Family's "Wait No More" conferences[6] and the Christian Alliance for Orphans annual summit.[7] John tells of God's heart for orphans and vulnerable children, but, he told me, "It is the Holy Spirit's job to recruit. I'm just an advocate."

John's concern, however, is that he's observed many Christian parents fall into a mindset of trying to protect their children so much that they are afraid that taking in orphans would ruin their biological kids. "Parents act as if they think their children are born perfect, and it is their job to get them to adulthood in that same state. But children are born with a sinful nature—they start out not like Jesus in a world not like Jesus," he told me.

"Kids need protection from themselves as much as other stuff out there and caring for kids without a family can develop kids for success in life because they grow up thinking about someone besides just themselves." In Paul's metaphor in Ephesians, they see themselves as part of God's big building project.

## DISCUSSION AND REFLECTION

- The foster-care system tries to keep children with their biological family if at all possible. Have you known instances where this was beneficial to children? Harmful? Why is this principle important for foster or foster-adopt families to keep in mind?
- The Moores have Native American, Hispanic, Cambodian, Caucasian, and African American children. How might you counsel a family who has children representing several races?
- John Moore stated that parenting children of several different races has helped him better understand the gospel. How so?
- Read Ephesians 2. What does Paul say about gospel unity among diverse races?
- John Moore has spoken at conferences for Focus on the Family and the Christian Alliance for Orphans. Have you attended one of these kinds of conferences or spoken with someone who has? How was the conference helpful?

# 15

---◆---

# Racial Profiling and Forgiveness of Sin

D. J. Jordan worked on Capitol Hill from 2008–2018, serving as a congressional aide to Senator James Lankford of Oklahoma from 2015–2018. He formerly worked as a journalist for Fox News. D. J. is African American. While he was working for Fox News, D. J. lived with his wife and their young son in Prince George's County, Maryland, just east of Washington, DC. They owned a condo in an upper-middle-class neighborhood of condos and apartments. After running errands one cold January day and dressed down in a casual hooded Redskins sweatshirt, D. J. returned to his neighborhood, exited his car, and started walking toward his condo. Along the way, he heard a woman crying and looked to see her apartment door open. She was clearly in distress.

D. J. approached to see if he could help. After just a few steps, however, two unmarked police cars sped into the parking lot and slammed on the breaks in front of D. J. Three plain-clothed, undercover male police officers ran from the vehicles, two with

guns drawn and pointing at D. J. The officers were yelling at
D. J., but he couldn't understand what they were saying. "No
idea whatsoever, because I was scared to death!" D. J. told me.

He dropped to the ground and hid behind a car. Fright
led to flight. D. J.'s first thought was that he was caught in the
middle of a gang or drug fight. "Probably after a minute, though
it seemed like an eternity, of these men screaming, I could understand what they were saying—that they were police—so I got
up with my hands above my head."

As D. J. rose from behind the car, the two undercover police
officers kept their guns aimed at D. J. and approached him.
"Who are you?" they demanded. "What are you doing here?
What's your relationship with this woman?" D. J. was able to
stutter in fear that he lived in the area and did not know the
woman. Handing the police his identification, D. J. waited in
shock as one police officer stood watch over him, gun drawn,
and another checked D. J.'s background. Though the police recognized that D. J. was innocent, they asked him to stay while
they finished investigating the incident at the woman's apartment. "That episode—I can't describe how scared I was and how
much it changed my life. I have never been in trouble with the
law, never even experimented with drugs. I was working [a very
visible job] at Fox News and I was *still* profiled as being a drug
dealer!" D. J. said.

## The African American Foster-Care Crisis

A few years after the profiling incident, D. J. and his wife,
Glorya, began to volunteer at a crisis pregnancy center in the pro-
life ministry of their church. In time, D. J. became a volunteer

board member of that center. As they counseled with people who faced unplanned pregnancies, those men and women asked if D. J. and Glorya were willing to adopt. Many of the people D. J. and Glorya ministered to were African American, and they would comment to the Jordans that there were not many families of color adopting children. "It really stood out to us—we need to be a part of this solution," D. J. told me.

D. J. put his journalist skills to work and researched the plight of kids without parents. "We did general research trying to find out the number of orphans worldwide, specifically in the United States. We looked into the process of adopting domestically and internationally. Then we started researching foster care." That was the tipping point. "It was like something hit us square in the face," he said. "There is a crisis in the foster-care system in America—and it's not like it is in some foreign continent. It is right in our own backyard!" Understanding the hardships of so many vulnerable children right in their own community sharpened the Lord's call upon D. J. and Glorya to foster with a view to adopting out of the foster-care system. The Jordans have fostered several children and adopted one child out of foster care.

What gripped the Jordans was the racial disproportionality in the foster-care system. The most recent United States census data for 2016 to 2017 reveals that African American children enter foster care at rates much higher than those of other races.[1] While those identifying themselves as white/Caucasian comprise 60 percent of the United States population, they make up 44 percent of kids in foster care. So the percentage of white/Caucasian kids in state custody is 16 percent lower than the representative population in the culture at large. The second largest racial demographic in the United States, non-white/Hispanics, comprise 18 percent of the population. The population of non-white/Hispanic children in foster care represents about their population rate in the United States. Roughly 21 percent of kids in foster care are non-white/Hispanic. However, children of black/African American descent make up 23 percent of kids in foster care while the black/African American population is just 13 percent of the total population. One in four children in foster care is black/African American while just one in ten people in the United States is black/African American. But D. J. insists that national data analysis like this reveals just part of the picture: "In many urban areas, 60 percent of kids in foster care are black."

These data have practical implications. In *Orphanology*, Tony Merida and Rick Morton shared the story of Page and Ashely Brooks's desire to adopt.[2] A social worker shared with the Brookses that if they wanted a Caucasian baby, it would likely be ten months to one year before they would become parents. But if they wanted a black or mixed-race baby, they could have one as soon as the next day. Why the difference? Most white couples want white babies and few black parents in their location were adopting.

Why this racial disparity? While a number of factors might explain the disproportionately high number of African American children in the foster-care system in the United States, D. J. points to three factors. While serving on the Virginia State Board of Social Services, D. J. observed the link between criteria that prompt social workers to pull kids from a home (neglect, poverty, and crime) and communities below the poverty line.

First, there is a direct connection to low-income communities having more children placed in foster care because domestic neglect and abuse is higher in economically impoverished communities. So in many states, minority communities have disproportionately higher rates of poverty than the general population. Therefore, more minority kids end up in foster care in those states. Since economically impoverished communities are also home to more minorities than those that are primarily Caucasian, it makes sense that more minority kids would be placed in foster care.

Second, "when a Child Protective Services representative visits a low-income neighborhood with a high crime rate, they are quicker to remove a suspected abused child from the home compared to a middle class neighborhood, because they may have a predetermined view of the poor community's history of crime," D. J. told me. High crime rates and poverty place kids in a vulnerable position—and many high-crime-rate, impoverished neighborhoods are disproportionally African American.[3]

Third, "social workers have a more difficult time recruiting families to foster children of color, especially boys." Since fewer families will foster or adopt African American boys, those boys remain in the system of short-term foster care or group homes until they age out at eighteen. Since a disproportionate number of African American boys do not have a stable father figure to shepherd them through their teen years, these young men are vulnerable to a criminal lifestyle. If a young man does not have a dad to teach him the value of self-discipline, hard work, respect for women, and the danger of narcotics, then we should not be surprised when fatherless young men begin to practice and identify with illegal activity.

# The African American Adolescent Male, the Local Police Department, and the Church

For months after D. J. was profiled that cold January day several years ago, he had nightmares and had to fight bitterness for nearly a year. Yet he supports the police. "We need to teach our children to honor the authorities," he said.

At the 2018 Christian Alliance for Orphans Summit, D. J. joined many others to equip a primarily Caucasian audience in parenting their African American foster or adopted children.[4] The conversation quickly turned to how parents might help black boys and young men grow into productive citizens in Christ. This panel of leaders helped the audience understand the need to have "the talk" with their sons. This is not the talk about sex; it is the talk about what to do when a young black man is pulled over by a police officer. The panel noted that black boys sometimes look older than they are, in comparison to white boys, and are sometimes mistaken by police for being older. Police may think they are dealing with someone in their late twenties when the boy is sixteen. The pullover protocol a black male should follow runs something like this: roll down the window and put hands out the window or in clear sight on the dashboard; ask permission to move; explain actions as they are being made so the officer(s) is in no way surprised; be sure not to back talk in any way.

Educating our children for these possibilities is a powerful way the church can help. The church is a unique institution in that we are concerned both for the rule of law and for the plight of the disadvantaged. In Romans 13, Paul established principles that inform even the modern discussion about police authority.

The church upholds the rights of police to enforce the laws of a society. "Government is God's servant for your good," Paul explained (Rom. 13:4, HCSB). Paul continued his argument in Titus 3:1–8 by stating that the church is to be submissive to the government because rebellious behavior does not befit the gospel of grace and salvation in Christ.

Peter's worldview reflected Paul's. In 1 Peter 2, the apostle argued that the church is to honor governmental authorities because in doing so, the church shows itself to be a peaceful institution. The peaceful, submissive behavior of the church demonstrates the peaceful gospel the church has received. Local churches are uniquely positioned to address racial tensions in our culture because the gospel shapes our thinking about ethnicity and the role of government to enforce the law. And churches that participate in orphan care are on the front lines of the conversation.

*Local churches are uniquely positioned to address racial tensions in our culture because the gospel shapes our thinking about ethnicity and the role of government to enforce the law.*

In fact, D. J. has seen many white parents who foster or adopt minority kids become advocates for racial justice. "They see race issues from a different perspective. I think a lot of parents go there pretty quickly, to be honest with you. Especially white suburban moms who are adopting black children—they become warriors for racial justice. You don't mess around with them—they are momma bears! They come out of their shells for racial justice." As D. J. and Glorya learned, many of the kids who need our help and compassion are African American. Orphan-minded churches can listen with open ears and hearts to both minority communities and law enforcement, advocating for justice and the rule of law. As we partner with our church to foster or adopt, we provide homes for kids and seize the cultural moment to show the watching world the power of the gospel.

## DISCUSSION AND REFLECTION

- D. J. and Glorya Jordan became burdened by the number of African American children in foster care. How do the statistics presented in this chapter impact you?
- According to D. J., what factors contribute to such a high proportion of minority kids in the foster-care system?
- What might your church do to help those families so that children are not removed from their parents?
- Read Romans 13 and 1 Peter 2. What do Paul and Peter state about the role of government and law enforcement?
- D. J. Jordan had to overcome an instance of profiling that could have been deadly. What helped him to forgive the officers? Why is he still pro-law enforcement?
- In what ways can you work to better the relationship between law enforcement and your community?

# Part 6

◆

# ORPHAN CARE AND THE SEX-TRAFFICKING EPIDEMIC

(Special Note: chapters
16–18 contain graphic content)

# 16

## Why the Local Pimp Does Not Want You to Foster or Adopt

Within two months of working in the forensics division of the Sexual Assault Nurse Examiner (SANE) unit at Children's Mercy Hospital in Kansas City, Missouri,[1] Heidi Olson realized that many of the girls she examined were actually victims of human trafficking.[2] SANE nurses investigate cases of suspected assault and collect evidence for law enforcement.[3] When law enforcement officials bust a prostitution ring or apprehend a child on the run, they take the kids to the hospital for evaluation.

It turns out that trafficking victims have a common history, a pattern or formula, which Heidi first saw in the case of a sixteen-year-old girl. This girl had been in a group home in the custody of the state. She ran from her group home but not from social media. Through Facebook, she met a group of traffickers who promised her food, shelter, and safety. Having earned this girl's trust, they were able to move her from Missouri to Indiana where they put her to work selling herself. Police in Indiana arrested an older girl she was with and realized that this particular girl was a missing person and returned her to Missouri. When Heidi examined this young woman, she had four sexually transmitted diseases, genital trauma, cigarette burns, and signs of general physical abuse. "This did not seem like your average sexual assault case—not that there is an average—but this seemed extreme, repeated," Heidi told me. "I suspected she was being trafficked." Heidi called law enforcement, the FBI, and DCFS—but no one came to check the case. She had to discharge the girl to the care of the girl's grandmother, only to discover later that the girl ran away from her grandmother that night and was being trafficked again.

That case ignited within Heidi a desire for justice. "I told myself, *We cannot let this happen again*," Heidi said. "Every system that is supposed to help these kids has failed." Today Heidi is the SANE program coordinator at Children's Mercy. She teaches nurses how to recognize trafficking and works with agencies to break the cycle of abuse as early in a child's life as possible. Heidi also trains nurses, law enforcement, and community agencies to recognize the formula of sex trafficking, a pattern she has seen repeatedly since that first young girl's case.

## The Sex-Trafficking Pattern

Heidi learned that the common history sex-trafficking victims share is apparent in five factors.[4]

First, these kids are often born to parents whose lives are characterized by criminal behavior. Sometimes this criminal behavior includes sexual abuse by the parents or an extended family member. Heidi told me that Children's Mercy sees an average of thirty-five to forty children a month who have been sexually assaulted (a staggering number, but small compared to the three hundred per month that Children's Mercy reports for both sexual and physical abuse). Since sexual forensic evidence can only be collected within a five-day window, these are just the verifiable assaults. "Previous sexual assault is a big risk factor for being trafficked," Heidi said. "In our community, there are hundreds of kids ripe for trafficking."

Second, besides sexual abuse, illegal drug use frequently surfaces in these families, creating a handle for sex traffickers to later lure these kids, who have been exposed to those substances at an early age. In the family of origin and extended kin, illegal drugs are esteemed. Drugs equal money, clout, esteem, and power. Drugs are thus seen as valuable, desirable, and necessary.

Third, as a result of these criminal activities in the immediate family, these kids are placed in foster care. Kids who are trafficked nearly always became wards of the state early in their lives. In fact, Heidi told me that every victim of child trafficking she has treated was at one time a ward of the state. One hundred percent. "I am sure there are kids who are trafficked who haven't been in foster care, but in my experience, they almost always are or have been," she said. The criminal behavior of the family of origin results in the child being removed from the home and placed in foster care or group homes. Often the foster placements are with extended family, labeled "kinship placements." The problem? These family members often practice the same dangerous activities as the biological parent(s) the children were originally removed from. Abuse—including further sexual abuse—and drugs follow these kids from one family member to another. This prompts DCFS to step in a second, third, or fourth time. With each consecutive placement, the child becomes less attached to the foster home.

Fourth, the one stable factor in these kids' lives is social media. Having begun an online presence, they make connections, chat, offer nuggets of personal information, and reveal themselves through both images and words. And pimps are social media experts.

*Pimps are social media experts.*

Fifth, kids who become trafficked have run away from their foster home placement or their group home.[5] Kids on the run are vulnerable. They are desperate to avoid getting reported to DCFS as that would restart the cycle of foster placements or group home assignments. "Imagine you are fourteen. You are living on the street—or attempting to. You can't even meet your own basic needs," Heidi explained. Where might these kids find shelter? Yes, the trusted figure on the other end of that social media connection.

On the street, these kids have no money and no protection. In this compromised state, they become increasingly susceptible to two often interrelated forces: pimps and drugs. Since the child on the run likely has a history that includes the idea that drugs are money, identity, and security, they become easy targets. Pimps know this. The men, women, and organizations that traffic kids for money know that these children are candidates for addiction. Drugs are an extremely persuasive force in the hands of criminals preying on former foster kids who have run away.

How do these children fall victim so easily? Some pimps are

reported to have seemed caring and genuine—at first. "These traffickers are not thugs," Heidi said. "They have a strategic business model." Pimps start by making promises and fulfilling them. They promise their victims food and shelter, take them to the movies, buy them a cell phone, get them tattoos. Pimps provide an identity for vulnerable kids. And as the pimp earns trust, the pimp begins to break the kids in for sexual service.

Part of this scenario is nearly always drugs. Get the kids hooked on drugs and the promise of drugs will persuade them to give themselves away sexually. To establish in the kids' mind that they are the property of the pimp, sometimes the pimp will move them to a different location. These kids are forced to live in drug houses in town and cities they do not know, and they are sold day after day. Heidi noted that the Indy 500, the Super Bowl, military bases, and truck stops are destination points for pimps when they want to take their girls on the road.[6] Since these pimps need buyers, they take their kids (supply) to their highest concentration of customers (demand). What keeps the kids from running again? Fear, threats, and drugs. "Meth is the trafficker's drug of choice," Heidi told me.

What might break this cycle in a kid's life? Death, or more commonly, severe disease or genital bleeding. A trafficked kid with a sexually transmitted infection (STI, as they are currently labeled) comes to a hospital emergency room late at night—and nurses like Heidi are called in to do an examination.

The average age of trafficked kids who come to Children's Mercy is twelve to thirteen years old. But Heidi has seen children as young as two and several in their mid-teens. When these nurses examine these children, they get one shot at helping them. "The vast majority of them, we never see again," Heidi said. "We have this little moment in time when our worlds collide, and I think there is this sense of urgency that we need to intervene *now* to help."

## The Good Samaritan and Vulnerable Children

Fortunately, there is hope. You and I can bring vulnerable kids into our homes with the goal of giving them an identity with us and in Christ so they don't identify with drugs and pimps. Prevention is the best tactic for fighting the foster-care-to-sex-trafficking pipeline. Welcoming kids who might be trafficked is applying Jesus' famous parable of the Good Samaritan in Luke 10:25–37 to our mission.

> *Prevention is the best tactic for fighting the foster-care-to-sex-trafficking pipeline.*

When a Jewish scribe asked Jesus what he must do to inherit eternal life, Jesus answered with his own question, "What is written in the Law?" (Luke 10:26). Jewish scribes were power brokers in Jesus' day. In a culture of illiteracy, they could not only read and write, they were professional interpreters of the Jewish Scriptures. This scribe displayed his training by citing two foundational Old Testament passages, Deuteronomy 6:9–25 and Leviticus 19:18, telling Jesus that these texts in the law required Israelites to love God with all their lives and to love others as themselves. Jesus affirmed the scribe's answer saying, "Do this and you will live" (Luke 10:28).

But the scene shifted when this scribe asked Jesus to specify exactly who his neighbor was. This scribe was looking for a way to limit the demands he would place on himself and others in regard to caring for those in need around them. Jesus took up the lawyer's question by offering the parable of the good Samaritan.

The parable begins with a nondescript man quickly becoming vulnerable to the point of death. This man left Jerusalem and as he was heading to Jericho, he was robbed, beaten, and left for dead. It is not a stretch to let this robbed, wounded man represent kids in foster care. Kids who have been abused and exposed to drugs, whose parents are incarcerated, differ little from the half-dead man in Jesus' parable. As Jesus crafted the scene, both a priest and a Levite passed by and offered this man no help. These two religious figures did not obligate themselves to this man despite his vulnerable condition. They did not believe themselves responsible to care for this man even in his desperate state. It was the Samaritan—one whose Jewish lineage lacked the purity of a priest or a Levite—who broadened his shoulders to care for the wounded man.

Jesus concluded His parable by questioning the scribe, "Which of these three do you think proved to be a neighbor to the man who fell into the robbers' hands?" (Luke 10:36). Jesus led the scribe to understand that we should be more concerned with being neighborly to the vulnerable than categorizing who is or who is not worthy of our care. As New Testament commentator Darrell Bock put it, "The issue is not thinking about who someone else is, but what kind of a person I am."[7]

As believers partner together in their churches to act neighborly to vulnerable children, we can break the sex-trafficking pattern at step three—before children are sold for sex! Churches cannot prevent criminally minded parents from having children nor can we prevent the abuse some kids may endure early in life. But if DCFS is swamped with foster-parent applications from your church and mine, social workers are less likely to continue to place kids in kinship placements where the cycle of abuse might lead to a runaway and the sex-trafficking formula operating in another child's life. And in light of the increasing influence of pornography in our culture, which has a strong connection to trafficking, our churches will need to be more willing to care for vulnerable kids in the future.

## Where Does This All Begin?

Many don't realize the pornography and trafficking connection. But Heidi told me, "That is where it all begins. Pornography gives permission. It objectifies women to the point of being tools for sexual gratification." Heidi noted that the pervasive influence of pornography is affecting younger and younger boys. The average age of a sexual assault perpetrator identified at Children's Mercy is eleven to fifteen years old.[8] These are not the (usually) men purchasing sex but perpetrators who are committing assaults against kids generally their own age. Where do these preteen boys learn of aggressive sexual activity? Pornography. And if boys act this way as preteens, they are likely to keep pimps in business

> *From a business perspective, pornography is a pimp's marketing tool—and since sexual imagery pervades our culture, pimps do not have to pay an advertising agency.*

later in their lives as their demand grows stronger. From a business perspective, pornography is a pimp's marketing tool—and since sexual imagery pervades our culture, pimps do not have to pay an advertising agency.

But pornography is not just a contributing factor in the sex-trafficking epidemic, it is also often the end result of trafficking. According to Heidi, nearly all the trafficking victims she has treated report at some point being filmed as they were sold. Pimps see vulnerable kids as supply for the demand of their clientele. But the church offers something better: the church has the supply for the emotional and relational brokenness kids without parents desperately need. We have the chance to be the good Samaritan to kids robbed of a family.

---

## DISCUSSION AND REFLECTION

- What stands out to you from Heidi's work?
- How might your church help people see that pornography has real, human victims?
- What steps might your church take to increase believers' awareness of their need to foster or adopt vulnerable girls who might became the prey of a pimp?
- Read Luke 10:25–37. How might foster care or adoption reflect the work of the good Samaritan?
- In what other ways can your church demonstrate compassion to victims of sexual exploitation and sexual sin in our culture?

# 17

## The Pimp's Chief Operating Officer: A Woman

Rhi, as I will call her, loves to hit the city streets with her friends on weekend nights. While out on the town for them might include dinner or a club, entertainment is not on the agenda. Rhi and company walk the concrete and asphalt looking for victims of sex-trafficking. Sometimes Rhi and her friends visit strip clubs to build relationships with the women employed there.

Rhi is a nursing administrator, employed by a multistate health-care system where she oversees policy and identifies how the system can deliver treatment more effectively. She puts her nursing skills to work volunteering with a local ministry that seeks to identify, care for, and rescue victims of sex-trafficking. "It takes a lot of time and effort to get to know these victims of trafficking," Rhi told me. "They see so many people who want to take from them, use them, that they have a very low level of trust."

Just because Rhi is a thoughtful, patient woman with a heart for the vulnerable does not necessarily incline a trafficked victim to trust her. "These girls and young women have been used not just by a pimp—or pimps—but by women as well." Rhi explained that a "successful" pimp will have at least one female employee who is normally at the lowest end of the leadership structure but placed over the girls and women. She is a designated house mom for sex operations. This woman is totally devoted to the pimp, ironically, because she is no longer serviceable on the street. Since no customer would be willing to buy time with her, she must earn her keep another way. Once a pimp identifies a girl or young woman as a potential "employee," this lead woman will befriend the new staff, serving as a mentor. Because this structure is so common on the streets, it may take Rhi months to convince a trafficked victim that Rhi is not working for a pimp.

## A Well-Established Business Model

FBI reports confirm Rhi's observation. In 2016, the FBI-led Toledo Child Exploitation Task Force in cooperation with the Lima, Ohio, police department, arrested seven individuals involved in running a prostitution ring of under-age girls. Those arrested included two leading male figures, one of these men's girlfriend, and his mother. Reporting on the case, FBI special agent Devon Lossick said, "Members of the conspiracy would go after vulnerable and trusting young girls—usually runaways and others estranged from their families—by promising them money and then coaxing them into posing for sexually explicit photos."[1] These photos became advertisement on adult websites. The ringleaders of this prostitution business would provide contact info and ways that customers could arrange for meeting an adolescent of choice—even across the Ohio state line into Indiana.

When Rhi establishes enough trust with a trafficking victim, she patiently moves through a series of questions to see what she can do to help. Would the victim be willing to meet at a restaurant with Rhi and one of Rhi's friends? Is she interested in getting out of trafficking? Would she like to hear about other victims who have gotten out? What kind of a treatment program would she be willing to enter? Would she be willing to relocate?

Since women who run from their pimp and enter a treatment program some distance away are more likely to finish the treatment and successfully reintegrate into society, Rhi has relocation in the back of her mind as her relationship with a victim progresses.

But the first piece of information Rhi needs is the victim's age. Different scenarios develop for women under eighteen than those eighteen and older. For those over eighteen—even if they are slaves of a pimp—payment for sex is a prosecutable offense. But prosecution is rare, Rhi told me, since many of these women also work in more "legitimate" sex careers like dancing at strip clubs or participating in pornography. Their prostitution is more occasional and flies under the radar. Occasionally, a coordinated FBI and local law enforcement sting will uncover a prostitution network that leads to arrests of both prostitutes and the men and women employing them. Rhi and her friends work to free these women before they are caught and prosecuted—or worse, before they become so engrossed in a sex-for-payment lifestyle that they never leave it.

When a woman wants out, the first twenty-four hours are the most crucial. "This is our window of time," Rhi said. If an agency can convince a prostitute to enroll in a treatment program in an area far removed from her place of employment,

getting her on the way on day one, the chances of her going back
on the streets diminish greatly.

But what about girls who are under eighteen? Rhi shared
with me that four common themes run through the lives of girls
she has encountered on the streets. First, they came from a broken
family. Single parents and absent parents were the foundation of
their lives. Second, the brokenness of their family was directly
related to the absence of their father or a father figure. Third,
and often related to the second theme, these girls were sexually
abused as children. Dad's absence was often because authorities
removed him from the home. Other father figures walked in his
steps, present long enough to coerce and rape. Fourth, these girls
were placed in foster care or group homes.

And they run away. Many of these girls were initially placed
with extended family and abused or neglected there. Others
resisted the structure of the foster home, longing for freedom.
Though they were sexually abused in their family of origin or
other family placements, at least when they were not
being raped they were free to do as they pleased. Rhi
said that the average age a girl begins to sell herself
for sex is twelve years old. "They will run back to what
they know," Rhi stated.

*Churches can provide these girls with a relational grid that replaces the weakened social and emotional structures of their lives.*

The quality of foster homes often has some-
thing to do with children running. Believers partnering together
in their churches to foster children can provide an extensive

network of relationships to support vulnerable kids. Even at the structural level—setting the spiritual dynamics of Christianity aside for just a moment—churches can provide these girls with a relational grid that replaces the weakened social and emotional structures of their lives. But the spiritual dynamic can be set aside for only a moment—as we shall see below.

According to the National Center for Missing and Exploited Children (NCMEC), 15 percent of kids reported missing in 2017 were likely a victim of sex trafficking. Of that 15 percent, 88 percent were in the foster-care system when they were reported missing.[2] On the street, these girls are desperate for identity and love—and to stay clear of getting caught. While those eighteen and older are prosecutable, those younger than eighteen are taken into custody and placed in juvenile detention while they await a group home or a foster placement. Rhi said that in her experience, most girls survive two years on the street before authorities catch them. How do these twelve-year-old children make it? Remember that sex-trafficking house mom? She is the link between a pimp who employs the girl and the girl's most basic human needs. The sex-trafficking victims trust the woman who recruited them. Younger girls find their identity in working for the pimp's chief operating officer. She makes sure the younger girls get paid, get drugs—and get to work for the pimp.[3]

## The Woman at the Well and the Women on the Street

According to the Gospels, sexual promiscuity and the degradation of women are spiritual matters. The Gospels state that a relationship with Jesus Christ is humanity's greatest spiritual need.

So potent is a relationship with Jesus that He brings a sense of wholeness to other relationships as well. Even those with a sordid sexual past are healed and made whole by recognizing Jesus as the Messiah and receiving His message of forgiveness. Jesus' interaction with the Samaritan woman in John 4 speaks to vulnerable girls and women today.

Aware of the growing opposition from the Pharisees, Jesus headed north from Judea to Galilee. On the way, Jesus chose to pass through Samaria, where He stopped at a well and asked a Samaritan woman for a drink of water. Many Jews in Judea despised the Samaritans because the Assyrians had defiled their lineage after the exile (see 2 Kings 17:24–41). These foreigners intermarried with the descendants of Abraham, compromising Jewish purity forever. So when a Jewish man like Jesus dared to speak to her, let alone ask her for a favor like the hospitable act of drawing water, the woman was shocked.

Two things take place at once in this conversation. Jesus was revealing this woman's compromised sexual history, and He was revealing Himself as God's life-giving Messiah. Jesus told the woman that the daily routine of water drawing demonstrated the insufficiency of the well's water. It could not satisfy real thirst. Jesus, on the other hand, offered water that swells up in a person and satisfies forever (vv. 13–14). In what seems an initial faith-response, the woman requested that Jesus give her this water. Jesus seized the moment to help her acknowledge both her need for Him and His identity as the Messiah.

Jesus asked her to call her husband. She had no husband, she confessed—and Jesus miraculously recounted the details of her life story. More than just the woman's compromised ethnicity is noteworthy in John 4. This woman had a sordid moral past.

She'd had five husbands and the man she was currently with was not her husband. New Testament scholar Gary M. Burge observed, "She has doomed her reputation and broken the morals of her community."[4] Jesus exposed this woman as needing spiritual life, and He was revealed as the Messiah, the One who offers God's restorative goodness even to outsiders with sordid sexual histories.

The spiritual healing this woman received is a picture of what God does as we herald the message of the gospel. But we can also prevent some of the sexual brokenness in our culture by interrupting the foster-care-to-sex-trafficking supply chain. As we provide vulnerable kids with a stable family and display the identity and healing that Jesus offers, we decrease the chances that kids become victims of a pimp's business ambitions. For a pimp, kids are tools. For God and us, they are treasures.

## From Street to Home

When Rhi meets a teenage girl on the street, she tries to connect with her through genuine interest and patience. "It takes a lot of time," she said. In one recent situation, Rhi's patience led to a long-term mentoring relationship. The girl ran away from home when she was thirteen and by fourteen she was being sold. She told adults around her that the twenty-six-year-old man who accompanied her in public was her boyfriend. This girl endured the four common themes Rhi noted above, culminating in an arrest at age sixteen during an FBI raid. That's when Rhi befriended this girl. Her patience began to warm this girl—she wanted to be around Rhi as much as Rhi wanted to be around her. When it came time for social services to place this girl, she asked if she

*For a pimp, kids are tools. For God and us, they are treasures.*

could live with Rhi. As a single woman with no intentions of becoming a licensed foster parent, Rhi had work to do. She enrolled in foster-care classes and began fostering that young woman.

You and I may never be called to do what Rhi does—go out on the streets and work with victims there—but if we are serious about being followers of Christ, we are all called to get involved. The New Testament writers are clear on that.

"These kids need patience—time, time, time, grace, and understanding," Rhi said. Traits the church is unique to offer. The church is the life-giving force of Jesus. The church offers living water to girls whose souls have been dried up by abuse and neglect and the sex trade.

As we welcome vulnerable kids into our homes, we decrease the chances that children will become victims of a pimp's exploitation. When I consider what could have become the lifestyle of my adopted daughters, I cringe. I cringe at the thought of a pimp's lead woman lying to and manipulating these girls who are now my daughters. And I rejoice that today my daughters are under the good and honoring influence of my wife and the women of my church. I rejoice that my adopted daughters attend Sunday school, ladies' Bible studies, regular kids' ministries, and the weekly small group that meets in my home. I rejoice when my adopted daughters do cartwheels in the hallway of the seminary where I teach (when they are with me at my office later in the evenings!). The best tactic for fighting sex trafficking is to prevent it. That's what we can do as we partner together in our local churches to foster or adopt.

---

## DISCUSSION AND REFLECTION

- Why would patience be important when working with a victim of sex trafficking?
- Describe the business model of a pimp. Why would a lead woman be a valuable employee?
- What is the business of the church when it comes to victims of sex trafficking?
- Read John 4. How would you describe Jesus' attitude toward the sexual sin of the Samaritan woman?
- What might your church do to help those in your congregation who feel called to foster or adopt teen girls who have been trafficked?

# 18

◆

# The Family of God as the Place to Belong

Dr. Karen Countryman-Roswurm is the executive director of the Center for Combating Human Trafficking (CCHT) at Wichita State University. Though she is not yet forty years old, she has worked to combat human trafficking for twenty-three years. Did you catch that? Karen began helping vulnerable teens and young women when she was a teen.

Due to a tragic family situation, Karen was orphaned at thirteen. From thirteen to sixteen, she was legally in foster care but essentially lived on the streets, running away from foster and group homes, experimenting with drugs, living in fear of being trafficked. As a juvenile, she realized she had no say over what happened to her, so at sixteen, she petitioned the state to be recognized as an adult. She felt that would allow her some sense of safety. The judge concurred with Karen's argument and emancipated her. Karen was on her own, free to live in her own apartment, free from the foster-care system.[1] At sixteen, while most teenagers are focused on their own lives, Karen began to look out for her peers who were prey to traffickers.

Karen began working for the Wichita Children's Home street outreach program.[2] "When we would walk to or from the Wichita Children's Home to a school or another location, it was apparent that people pursued us," Karen told me. By "people," Karen meant pimps.

While Karen was working with the Wichita Children's Home street outreach program, the University of Nebraska hired her to assist researchers in a project called the Midwest Longitudinal Study of Homeless Adolescents.[3] The project tracked runaway and homeless youth in six cities in Missouri, Iowa, Nebraska, and Kansas in hopes of learning about the effects trauma has on mental health. Someone like Karen would be no small asset for their research. Over the next four years, she tracked forty runaways, half of whom were in the foster-care system.

In 1998, while doing this research, a particular experience shaped Karen's sense of calling. She witnessed a trafficker beat one of the girls she was monitoring for the study. The fifteen-year-old girl was five months pregnant. When Karen pulled up to the apartment to interview her, the girl ran toward Karen for help. She was able to get to Karen's car, open the passenger-side door, and get in, but the pimp jumped on her in the front seat. He beat this girl right in front of Karen. In God's providence, a police officer was on lunch break in the area, noticed what was going on, and arrested the pimp.

At that time, the laws in Kansas allowed the State to prosecute a man for domestic violence against a woman even if that woman did not choose to press charges. But since the law categorized this girl as a juvenile delinquent prostitute and not a victim of domestic violence, if she choose not to press charges, neither would the State. And this girl did not want to take legal action against the man who had just beaten her. Why? Karen explained that though, from the outside, this girl's life seemed a wreck, it was actually an improvement from her family of origin. As a victim of trafficking, this girl had more choice over who she had sex with than when she was in her home with her family. There her dad raped her; her brothers raped her; her dad sold her to his friends and his brothers. All this to pay for his drug habits and the monthly rent. "What can be stolen can be sold," Karen said. "This girl had been in a boot camp preparing her for this further experience of commodification since the time she was really young."

Today as executive director of the CCHT, Karen works to shape both policy and people. She has lobbied Kansas lawmakers to recognize exploited youth not as criminal perpetrators but as victims.[4] And Karen has continued in direct intervention with sex-trafficking victims as well. The CCHT works with the Office of Juvenile Justice Detention Prevention of the US Department of Justice[5] to provide training across the country. The CCHT model taught at these events focuses on the power of healthy relationships.[6] "One of the greatest truths is that no matter how smart you are, no change can happen outside of a transformational relationship," Karen said. Healthy relationships prevent kids from being exploited. Healthy relationships have the power to help victims of sexual exploitation transform their lives.

According to Karen, kids in foster care are accustomed to sharing personal information with people they do not know all that well. The result? These kids are vulnerable to being manipulated by adults with an agenda. Who might that be? Traffickers. How do traffickers manipulate? By promising kids identity and

*No amount or theory of care will help these kids until they are surrounded by people committed to them in loving relationships.*

family or by threatening them with physical harm or loss of freedom. Attorney Michael Dolce agrees: "Their worth is what the abusive caregiver gets from them, whether simply a paycheck from the state or their bodies for sex, as happened to some of my clients. This conditions them to be subservient to pimps—giving all they have in exchange for essential needs, like food and shelter."[7]

That is why, Karen argues, that no amount or theory of care will help these kids until they are surrounded by people committed to them in loving relationships.[8] The goal of these relationships? Helping kids think in new ways. Kids who are vulnerable to traffickers or who have been sold for sex need patterns of thinking that are not based in fear or anger. "Even if we were to give kids a mansion and money, it would not get them off the street if we cannot get them to think differently about who they are and how they might live a better way," Karen told me. Her goal at the CCHT is to recreate the relational narrative of these kids so they might be able to make progress with housing, vocation, and education. "If we don't deal with the emotional and relational center of that child's soul, no amount of externals will help."

## Christianity Is a
## Relational Religion

What group in society has the relational capacity for vulnerable
boys and girls ages six to
twelve, who are prime targets of sex traffickers? The
church does by offering
the kinds of relationships
these children need. Why?
Because Christianity is a
relational religion. Looking at just Paul's letter to
the church in Ephesus as
an example, we can see that
Christianity is character-

> *Christianity is a relational religion. . . . Christianity is characterized by a vertical relationship with God and horizontal relationships inside and outside of the church.*

ized by a vertical relationship with God and horizontal relationships inside and outside of the church.

In Ephesians, as throughout the New Testament, the vertical relationship individual believers and the church have with
God is to influence all horizontal relationships. This framework
of relationships is so powerful that it has the capacity to stabilize
kids who might easily fall prey to traffickers. Before following the
vertical and horizontal relationship grid in Ephesians 5:1–6:4, I
want to note that what Paul described here is not a super-spiritual
picture of Christianity. This is not just for the elite Christians
or church leaders. This is normal, everyday, vanilla Christian
teaching. The character of a person's relationships always demonstrates their beliefs.

Ephesians 5:1, "Be imitators of God, as beloved children,"

echoes Ephesians 4:1, "I, the prisoner of the Lord, implore you to walk in a manner worthy of the calling with which you have been called." What God has done for the Ephesians individually and collectively, Paul wanted them to display to one another and to the world. And God has demonstrated His love in personal terms, through Christ's self-sacrifice for sin (5:2). How might believers display similar love for one another? Paul's concern in Ephesians 5 was that believers show God's love in the church through moral purity and uprightness. This very principle that Paul set out at the beginning of Ephesians 5 is what vulnerable kids in foster care need: loving interaction with adults that is not based on sex. Paul's concern for moral purity in the church compelled him to use a metaphor of light versus darkness to describe the spiritual condition of believers and non-believers. Since believers are "Light in the Lord" (v. 8), they are to walk in the light of moral goodness (v. 9), and expose "the unfruitful deeds of darkness" (v. 11).

Paul's teaching on marriage in Ephesians 5:22–33 expresses once again the vertical-to-horizontal perspective of Christianity. Husbands are to love their wives as Christ loved the church. Wives are to be subject to their husbands as unto the Lord. God's strong and abiding love for believers—this is what believers are to demonstrate to one another. This is especially so in the closest human relationship, marriage. Though no Christian marriage is perfect, on the whole, Paul described a framework of relationships empowered by God Himself. We cannot say that the church does not have the relational capacity to care for vulnerable kids who need strong, loving relationships and identity in a community of love. That is in fact what Paul exhorted the Ephesians to express in their parenting. When Paul commanded parents to raise their children "in the discipline and instruction of the Lord" (6:4), he wanted them to show God's loving, enduring character to their children as they progress through the various stages of life. Paul's goal was that as kids watch their parents, they see God. Believers and churches who practice such parenting can provide needy kids with relational attachments that prevent them from falling prey to the cheap-love substitute of getting a cell phone from a pimp.

## Run in the Fundraiser 5K *and* Open Your Home

Karen has seen how pimps' influence ruins years of life for young women. From her position at the CCHT, Karen understands both the personal and legal aspects of trafficking. She told me that sometimes trafficked teens on the street are charged not just with prostitution but also with the crime of trafficking. "These traffickers are not dumb, they are very smart," Karen said. Pimps will use the kids as recruiters with the result that *the kids*, not the pimps, are often charged with trafficking. The pimps use the kids' cellphones so that the pimps are not linked to an account that could lead to their arrest. What does this have to do with the church's responsibility for orphans? Of every single child the CCHT has worked with who has been charged with sex crimes, 100 percent of them were once in foster care. Many kids who were originally removed from their home because they were sexually abused are later incarcerated as registered sex offenders because their traffickers forced them to recruit and train other kids. Victims of sex-trafficking who are charged with sex-trafficking find themselves in a pit of spiritual, relational, and legal consequences. And these are not boys we're talking about. "These are all young girls," Karen told me.

Karen strongly believes that the church can change this reality. "We need you to rise up," she said. "We need you to open your homes—and if you cannot open your homes, at least wrap around those in your church who are opening their homes." Karen noted that many churches have become afraid of getting their hands dirty in the work of local missions. "We do just enough to feel good. Participating in a fund-raising run for a trafficking organization and getting a T-shirt is helpful, but the real need is for these kids to have healthy relationships in a healthy family and church community." Kids in foster care and orphanages are relationally vulnerable—and those in the sex-trafficking industry exploit that vulnerability for their own ends. But we know, as Paul described, the church is a foundation of stable relationships. Pimps offer a self-serving substitute of what only churches like yours and mine can provide. Let's put pimps out of business.

---

## DISCUSSION AND REFLECTION

- What most affects you about Karen Countryman-Roswurm's story?
- Broken families and unstable foster homes often serve as the soil from which pimps make a living. How might the church provide stability to foster families taking in high-risk kids?

- Read Ephesians 5:1–6:4. How would you summarize Paul's instruction about Christian relationships?
- How might the identity the gospel and the church provide meet the needs of kids desperate for belonging?
- Karen warns that many churches do just enough in missions to make themselves feel good but steer clear of getting messy and personally involved in the needs of the vulnerable, like orphans. How might you help your church avoid superficial missions work?

Part 7

◆

# ORPHAN CARE AND
# CHURCH LEADERSHIP

# 19

Leading from the Front

Jeff Dodge served as the teaching pastor at Cornerstone Church in Ames, Iowa, in Story County, from 1996 to 2019. By the end of Jeff's ministry there, most of the families licensed by the Iowa Department of Human Services (DHS) in Story County were part of Cornerstone Church. Story County even held foster-care and adoption licensure classes at the church.

So many people were involved in that ministry that Jeff was hard-pressed to walk through the foyer on a Sunday and not bump into someone with foster care or adoption as a part of their story. Why did Cornerstone's culture include such a robust orphan-care emphasis? It began with the pastoral staff.

They did not bring in a guest speaker or host a conference or preach a series of sermons on the topic. They personally began caring for vulnerable kids before the eyes of their watching congregation. On a short-term mission trip to Africa, one of the pastoral staff became burdened by the orphans he met there. He came home and did something about it. In short order, he and his wife pursued international adoption. As Jeff celebrated what

God was doing in that family, he kept running into DHS em-
ployees in his town. Jeff and his wife, Teresa, learned that though
Ames did not have visible orphanages like many countries in
Africa, their community had an orphan problem. So in 2007,
Jeff and Teresa enrolled in a DHS foster-care class. Cornerstone
church had two pastors personally engaged in orphan care.

Over the years, Jeff and Teresa have taken in six different
placements of children, including a couple of sibling sets. These
kids enjoyed the same family structure, spiritual nurture, and
church life that Jeff and Teresa provided their biological children.
In time, the Cornerstone family began to follow the example
of these pastors. The hallways, classrooms, and sanctuary of
Cornerstone—like the living rooms and dinner tables of church
members—have welcomed kids whose lives resembled a train
wreck. Orphans are needy and hard and desperate for compassion. Who but the church could help? God used the Cornerstone
church community to put some of these kids back on track.
Some families have even shared the parenting responsibility. A
family in their church adopted one of Jeff and Teresa's foster
placements.

What has motivated Jeff to stay engaged in orphan care even
through difficult seasons? The Scriptures. Throughout the Old
and New Testaments, God calls us to care for the more vulnerable
in our communities, Jeff told me. "In Deuteronomy 24, Moses
talks about this trio of needy people—the alien, the fatherless,
and the widow—with the emphasis to take care of these groups,"
Jeff told me. "Moses' conclusion is, 'Remember, you were a slave
in the land of Egypt. That's why I am commanding you these
things.' In effect, God says, 'Don't ever forget who you were

when I found you—therefore take care of the most vulnerable in your community.'" The prophets repeat those commands, "and once again indict the people of God for their refusal to care for that same trio of the alien, the fatherless, and the widow," he said. He referred to Jeremiah 7, in which the people were focused on the temple and ignored the needy around them. "Part of why Israel was sent into exile was because of their failure to care for this trio of vulnerable peoples."

Then Jeff turned to the New Testament and reflected on the specific place of church leadership in orphan-care ministry. While many recognize the church as God's means to care for orphans, who within the church might be equipped to personally take these children into their homes, giving orphans a nuclear family as well as connecting them with the resources of gospel-life in a local fellowship? His answer: "Pastors

> *We have to be activists in orphan-care ministry, we can't just lay heavy burdens on others to do what God has called His people to do.*

need to lead by example. We have to be activists in orphan-care ministry, we can't just lay heavy burdens on others to do what God has called His people to do," he told me. "If we urge the congregation to act but don't step out in front, we are at great risk before God, as well as being bad examples." He recommends that leaders don't simply roll out an orphan-care program, but they should enroll in a licensure class and take folks from the church with them! That seems like something Paul would say.

# Paul, Timothy, and
# Titus—Leading by Example

In 1 and 2 Timothy and Titus, Paul emphasized the need for
Timothy and Titus to follow his example so the church would
in turn follow their example,[1] thus providing the church with
a general pattern of behavior.[2] As Timothy and Titus modeled
integrity in their spheres, the congregations under their care had
observable patterns for practicing the faith. In Paul's strategy, as
the churches followed Timothy's and Titus's exemplary behavior,
the gospel would be defended against those who oppose the faith.
Though direct, personal orphan care is not specifically mentioned
in Paul's letters to these men, because orphan-care ministry is so
challenging, it is the kind of ministry that leaders must exemplify
if it is going to be done at all. And Paul had a lot to say about
leaders setting an example for those whom they lead.

In 1 Timothy 4, Paul urgently exhorted Timothy to counter
the deceptive spirit of the age by vigorously teaching Christian
doctrine and exemplifying behavior consistent with it. Why? Because these churches faced opposition from apostates and false
teachers—whose messages led to behavior that was inconsistent
with the gospel, but whom many outsiders understood to still be
associated with the church. If the watching world could not dis-
tinguish the behavior of the church from the behavior of those
who might be associated with it in name only, the pure message
of Christ would be compromised. Paul exhorted Timothy to set
forth, train himself in, command and teach, read forth, and give
himself to the gospel ministry. Weaved throughout these exhortations, Paul urged Timothy to "set the believers an example in
speech, in conduct, in love, in faith, in purity" (v. 12 ESV), even

to the degree that Timothy's progress could be seen by all in the church (v. 15).

At the outset of 2 Timothy, Paul described his relationship with Timothy like that of a father and his son. Paul urged Timothy to continue in ministry despite opposition, because he and Timothy had together shared in God's calling to salvation through the grace and glorious resurrection of Christ. Paul portrayed himself as one entrusted with this glorious gospel message (1:8, 11) and Timothy as one to whom Paul himself had entrusted the message of Christ. Paul commanded Timothy to set an example of endurance by holding "the pattern of the sound words" he had heard from Paul (1:13 ESV).[3] The potency of the gospel message, Paul reminded Timothy, would supply Timothy with the spiritual might necessary to live an exemplary life for the church—even in the midst of great opposition. The enduring potency of the gospel was effective to set Timothy as a pattern of endurance for the church of his day, and it has the same power to enable leaders to exemplary living in our age.

Through statements like, "charge them in the presence of God" (2:14) and, "present yourself approved to God" (2:15), Paul urged Timothy to carry out his ministry for an audience of One. Paul called Timothy to be an example of God-centeredness for the church. In light of the false teachers' and apostates' love for more talk and less action, as Timothy concisely spoke the truth of the gospel, he would be a model of trust in God (3:17–18; cf. Num. 16:5). Paul charged Timothy to flee the youthful passions of debate and pursue righteousness, faith, love, and peace from a pure heart (2:22). Timothy's truthful but peaceable ministry would establish an example for the church to be faithful with the

Word of God while at the same time avoiding a reputation of zealotry and rebellion (2:23–24).

Jeff and Cornerstone experienced this, as do many churches committed to ministries like orphan care. "Unbelievers are stunned by what we have done by taking in kids whose lives are a mess," Jeff told me. "Even if they think we are weird, right-wing evangelicals, they cannot deny the impact we are having for the good of our community."

In the midst of the contentious atmosphere of the first-century church, leaders that demonstrated calmness and love in proclaiming the Christian message would stand out from their opponents and the antagonistic temperament of those disputing simply for dispute's sake. By setting an example of truthfulness and humility, Timothy would be in a position to lead the church away from becoming a society of debaters and

> *Though not all of my neighbors will listen to me defend the gospel in sermons, they are able to see me care for my adopted daughters just as I do my biological children.*

toward being a people eager to demonstrate their gospel convictions by doing good works in love and the Spirit. And the same rings true today. Though not all of my neighbors will listen to me defend the gospel in sermons, they are able to see me care for my adopted daughters just as I do my biological children. They see the kind of peacemaking and justice that result from believing the gospel of peace.

Though Paul was concerned about what might lie ahead

for followers of Christ, he did not call Timothy to retreat or compromise. Rather, in accord with his command for Timothy to hold fast the sacred message of the gospel, Paul reminded him in 2 Timothy 3:10–11 that his own apostolic ministry had been marked by endurance of suffering even since the days before he met Timothy. Paul's reference to the cities of Antioch, Iconium, and Lystra would have brought back memories of the time when Paul's opponents stoned him and left him for dead (Acts 14:19–20)! Ultimately, however, Paul called Timothy to root his ministry in the pattern of life established by Jesus Himself (2 Tim. 3:15–16).

Themes of battling for the truth of the gospel in 1 and 2 Timothy and Titus are sometimes emphasized over Paul's exhortations for the church and its leaders to live peacefully. The theme of peace dominates 2 Timothy 2 and Paul's mindset in his letter to Titus. When Paul wrote to Titus, Titus was working on the isle of Crete—dominated by lazy and deceptive religious talkers. Against this backdrop, Paul was concerned for Titus to set an example of truthful speech and loving service for the church under Titus's watch.

Throughout his letter to Titus, Paul emphasized the need for the Cretan church to do good works. And in the midst of addressing various subgroups of the church in Titus 2, Paul directed attention specifically to Titus: "Show yourself to be an example of good deeds, with purity in doctrine, dignified, sound in speech which is beyond reproach, so that the opponent will be put to shame, having nothing bad to say about us" (vv. 7–8).[4] Titus's exemplary behavior, empowered by the grace of God in Christ and the presence of the Spirit, would serve to guide the church's response to the culture of depravity on Crete.

## The Effect of Example

Can you imagine attending a foster-care or adoption licensure class and mistaking it for a church small group gathering? What if you enrolled in one of the standard nine-week classes your state's DHS office offers, and when the teacher called roll on the first night, the roster was peppered with friends from your Sunday school class? That happened in Story County, Iowa, at Cornerstone Church.

Cornerstone has found that orphan care is a ministry that propels their church forward in church planting and social justice issues of all kinds. "That one ministry—orphan care—touches so many other facets of church life," Jeff told me. "It is a gateway ministry. For us, a beautiful by-product of orphan care is what it has done in our community."

When we partner with our local churches to foster or adopt, we exemplify the gospel message for our communities and benefit them. In loving kids, we show what God's love looks like. Never have our communities so needed demonstrations of God's love—and orphan care provides us an opportunity to show God's character while doing real, immediate good for our communities. And when church leaders personally involve themselves in orphan care, their example has a domino effect through their church to the world.

# DISCUSSION AND REFLECTION

- How did the orphan-care ministry begin at Corner-stone Church in Ames?
- Read 1 Timothy 4. What does Paul write about pastors being examples for the church? In what ways would you like to follow the example of your pastor(s)?
- In what ways do the concerns, interests, and burdens of pastors shape the ministry of a local church? How do the leaders of your church bring the congregation to participate in the ministry priorities they have set?
- How might you support the vision of your church leaders? How might your general support of church leaders further even your personal concern for orphan-care ministries?
- Based on Cornerstone's experience, in what ways can orphan-care ministry advance the impact of a church's general ministry in the community?

# 20

◆

# "If They Can Do It, Goodness, We Can Sure Do It!"

Having suffered the loss of miscarriage early in their marriage, Kevin and Lynette Ezell began to pray about expanding their family through adoption. While Kevin was pastoring Highview Baptist Church, in Louisville, Kentucky, he met the pastor of another church who had adopted a child from South Korea. After watching that pastor and his family through their adoption, Kevin and Lynette applied to adopt a child from South Korea as well. "That pastor, the pastor of a tiny church, changed our hearts and showed us what God had for our family," Lynette told me. Like so many hopeful couples, the Ezells were pierced when the South Korean adoption officials told them they were too young to be approved. But like so many couples whose hopes are pierced by childlessness, the Ezells watched as their marriage produced three children over the next several years. The Ezells filed away the adoption application and got busy parenting the children God had given them.

But God hadn't filed the idea away, and eventually one of their biological daughters prompted them to revisit the possibility of adoption. On her podcast, *The Adopting and Fostering Home*, Lynette shared, "Our middle school daughter began praying, and she really got a heart for adoption, and I remembered that file. We had never closed that door."[1] But the Ezells would recognize that the doors of adoption—especially international adoption—were yet difficult to open wide. So through perseverance, Keven and Lynette welcomed home a baby girl from China. As they raised her, the church body began to take notice. She would be the first of 120 children the members of their church welcomed between 2003 and 2010.

Not long after the Ezells adopted, the Lord brought to Highview another family, who had adopted a three-year-old girl from Ethiopia. The momentum had begun. Kevin spoke about adoption from the pulpit and the church held five-week classes a couple times a year in which those in the church interested in orphan care could get information and ask questions. Slowly the church's preschool resembled the United Nations. "I think because Kevin and I are incredibly transparent, we're just who we are, people looked to us, I really believe this, and said, 'If they can do it, goodness, we can sure do it,'" Lynette said on her podcast. God's adoption script for the Ezells had come full circle. They watched as a small-church pastor adopted from China. Then as Kevin was pastoring, his congregation watched as he and Lynette raised their biological and adopted children together in the church.

## Being Examples to the Flock

Paul knew the churches under the care of Timothy and Titus would be watching these men and the leaders they put in place. Paul tasked Timothy and Titus with identifying and evaluating local pastors who would shepherd and teach the church in the next generation. Considering Paul's numerous calls for them to be examples, it follows that they were to recognize as pastors those exemplifying the characteristics listed in 1 Timothy 3:1–7 and Titus 1:5–9. Likewise, Peter exhorted the elders in the churches under his care to be examples to the flock (1 Peter 5:3).

We can categorize Paul's list of pastoral qualifications in 1 Timothy 3:1-7 under three headings. Notice how these headings might supply the needs of orphans. First, Paul told Timothy to look for men who exemplified Christian integrity in the nearest spheres of life. This starts in the home. Potential pastors are to be "the husband of one wife" (v. 2). Likewise, they were to be men who managed their own families well, "for if someone does not know how to manage his own household, how will he care for God's church?" (v. 5 ESV). And the potential pastor's public character was to match his lifestyle at home. Timothy was to consider only men who were "sober-minded, self-controlled, respectable" (v. 2 ESV). Further, potential pastors were to have good reputations, so they would not be open to accusation and the devil's schemes (v. 7).

It is appropriate here to ask: What kind of parental environment do orphans need? In light of the fact that their lives have been turned upside down (sometimes on multiple occasions!) because of abuse and neglect, what kind of parent might be most helpful to an orphan? One of stable character, ideally, the stable character of a male head of household. Kids who have suffered loss or have been abused or neglected need authority figures who consistently maintain standards and structures inside and outside of the home. Since pastors *must* have this kind of character, it follows that they would qualify as a resource the church might call upon to help meet the needs of orphans.

The second qualification Paul stated was for potential pastors to have the ability to teach Christian doctrine (v. 2). The Christian faith is based on the unchanging doctrine of Jesus Christ, and pastors are to maintain that body of understanding, calling believers to trust the historical message and adjust their lives to it. This is not unrelated to the first qualification for pastoral leadership. Since the Christian message is a living truth, it is powerful enough to shape the behavior of those who have believed upon Christ. In Christianity, the content of the message shapes the character of those who believe. If orphans need anything, they need teachers. They need not just men but males who can teach them about the relationship between behavior and beliefs. Orphans need loving male authority figures who can get to their hearts and shepherd them in eternal truth. What pastors *must* do, orphans need.

> *Orphans need loving male authority figures who can get to their hearts and shepherd them in eternal truth. What pastors* **must** *do, orphans need.*

Finally, pastors must demonstrate hospitality to the needy (v. 2). New Testament scholar Philip Towner explained that in

Paul's day, the demand for leaders to demonstrate hospitality was not a call to mere social kindness. Because the church's commitment to Christ often placed believers in an impoverished socioeconomic position in the Roman Empire, "the practical and sacrificial sharing of one's home and minimal resources might mean survival for someone."[2] And children would have been especially vulnerable in an atmosphere of persecution.

David Platt observed that those who study the New Testament qualifications for pastoral leadership are often surprised when they find that many of these characteristics are to fill the lives of Christians generally. "This truth ought to weigh on anyone who aspires to lead in Christ's church, since a man cannot lead the church somewhere he is not going himself. Here's the bottom line: What will happen if the church imitates this leader?"[3]

Here again we find a point of contact with orphan care. Who in the church *must* be hospitable? The pastoral leadership. Who might need hosting? The needy—like orphans and widows, refugees and the marginalized. The circle of need expands here and there, but orphans would never not be included. Paul's explicit purpose statement for writing 1 Timothy synthesizes his concern for integrity of belief and practice in the church and underscores the need for elders to be examples of Christian behavior. In 1 Timothy 3:15 he explained, "I write so that you will know how one ought to conduct himself in the household of God, which is the church of the living God, the pillar and support of the truth."

These three themes provide an apt framework for understanding the similar list of qualifications Paul wrote in Titus 1:5–9. In light of the dark situation on Crete ("Cretans are always liars, evil beasts, lazy gluttons," Titus 1:12), it follows that those serving as pastors set the pace for good doctrine and good deeds. This is exactly what Paul called Titus to identify in potential elders. Pastors in Crete were to be men showing Christian behavior in private. They were to care for their families in such a way that if they extended the same patterns of leadership toward the whole church, they would be called good stewards of God's household. Potential elders were to have a track record of good behavior in public as well. Men who were quick-tempered, drunkards, violent, or greedy would contradict the message of Christ. They should be able to teach in such a way that they could refute those who opposed the gospel of Christ and the good works that flow from it. And those qualified were to have a reputation for good works toward the needy; they were to be hospitable and lovers of what is good.

Here again we have opportunity to see how the essential qualifications of pastoral leadership fit the needs of kids in crisis. Orphans are those who need models of consistent moral character, instruction from loving authorities, and arms that welcome them to a place of refuge. In business terms, we are dealing with supply and demand. The supply of pastoral leadership addresses the demands of orphan care at every point. This does not mean that every pastor must take in the needy, but if he is qualified to be a pastor, he would be qualified to participate in orphan care. David Prince, pastor of Ashland Avenue Baptist church in Lexington, Kentucky, and assistant professor of Christian preaching at The Southern Baptist Theological Seminary, connected the dots between Christian leadership and the needs of orphans when he wrote, "Churches, as outposts of the kingdom of Christ, must lead the way. Pastors, as the voice of Christ to their congregation, and fathers, as leaders in their families, must lead the way in adoption and orphan care. Rescued ex-orphans must be committed to leading the way in rescuing others, in seeing that others are granted an identity and an inheritance."[4]

Like Paul, Peter recognized that the elders of the church must set the pace for maintaining Christian doctrine and behavior in the face of opposition. At the conclusion of his first letter, Peter directed his attention to the elders of the church. He exhorted them to shepherd and oversee the flock among them by being examples (1 Peter 5:3). As I. Howard Marshall wrote, "The elders should be examples to the flock, demonstrating in their conduct of leadership the same qualities they wish to see in the congregation generally."[5] Peter listed this exhortation as the antithesis of the kind of domineering leadership that calls the congregation to act a certain way but does not model that behavior for them. Like Paul's, Peter's statements rest on the idea that the church at large requires visual patterns of Christian good works. If the church is to take up specific Christian activities to defend the Christian message before scoffers in the world, the elders must demonstrate such behavior so the believers under their care have an example to follow.

## A Fixable Problem

Kevin and Lynette Ezell's example at Highview Baptist Church established a pattern for many families to follow. In fact, Kevin and Lynette's example has been followed in their own family as both of their daughters have adopted children as well. Kevin and Lynette? In 2010, Kevin left Highview to serve as president of the North American Mission Board (NAMB) of the Southern Baptist Convention. Not long after, they added a Filipino boy to their family. His experience with adoption has brought

*"This is a fixable problem. Poverty is very hard to fix, but the foster-care problem—the church could eradicate it."*

a deeper level of concern to his work at NAMB as part of his role there is to encourage churches to step into compassion ministries like orphan care so believers can engage themselves in their communities and meet practical needs.

Regarding the orphan-care crisis in the United States, Kevin noted that it is more easily addressed than some other social-justice issues. "In the United States, there are roughly 425,000 children in the foster-care system and about 400,000 evangelical churches. It's not like every church has got to take three [kids]," he said. "This is a fixable problem. Poverty is very hard to fix, but the foster-care problem—the church could eradicate it."

But taking in kids in crisis is such a demanding task that if it is not modeled, it might not be done at all. And who might be qualified or have the maturity for such a task? Pastors who want their churches to take orphan care seriously know they must be out front—lest we set upon the flock a difficult task that we are unwilling to embrace ourselves.

# DISCUSSION AND REFLECTION

- Who first influenced Kevin and Lynette Ezell to adopt? Who first influenced you to think about fostering or adopting, or supporting those called to take children into their homes?
- How did God use their biological children to rekindle Kevin and Lynette's desire to adopt? How might parents who sense God's call to foster or adopt lead children they already have to join with them in bringing other children into their home?
- Do you have few or many companions walking the foster or adoption journey with you in your church? How might you increase the strength of this ministry?
- Read 1 Timothy 3 and Titus 1. How would the qualifications to pastoral leadership also serve to meet the needs of orphans?
- According to Kevin Ezell, how is the foster-care crisis a fixable problem?

# 21

◆

# Be the One?

Paul and Michelle Chitwood were ready to leave Rio de Janeiro and head back to the States. For just over a week, their team had been working in the slums outside of the city. They were busy leading a vacation Bible school, building a church, doing door-to-door evangelism, and providing medical and dental clinics. No matter the activity, a particular nine-year-old girl attached herself to Michelle. The mission trip concluded with a celebration night, at which the girl's mother appeared for the first time. In her Portuguese dialect, she frantically spoke to Paul and Michelle. Perplexed, the Chitwoods called for their interpreter to help them understand this woman's plight. "Take my little girl!" this girl's mother pleaded. "There's no hope for her here! Please take her!"

Though they were unable to honor the woman's request, it indelibly imprinted on their hearts, and they returned home burdened for kids like this girl—but even more so, for kids who had no parents at all. Several years later, Paul and Michelle adopted a girl from China, providing their two biological children with a younger sibling. When Paul served as the executive director of the Kentucky Baptist Convention from 2011–2018,[1] Paul took special interest in Sunrise Children's Services, formerly known as Kentucky Baptist Homes for Children, which "is Kentucky's largest nonprofit provider of services for children in crisis" and "serve[s] children from all of Kentucky's 120 counties."[2] Paul's goal was to get more Kentucky Baptists to think about fostering or adopting needy children right in their own state. Michelle assisted by initiating a campaign called "Be the One" to encourage at least one family from every Kentucky Baptist church to foster or adopt. The Chitwoods' hope was that for every one family who stepped up, the church would surround them with the support they would need.

In a short time, Michelle told Paul, "I think we need to be the one in our church. We need to consider fostering." In 2015, the Chitwoods became foster parents, and in 2018 adopted out of the Kentucky foster care system.

## What Is the Epistle of James About?

In his epistle, James addressed believers scattered because of persecution. The natural tendency of his audience was to complain against God, the world, and one another.[3] They were tempted to look to worldly resources to meet their needs.[4] But James exhorted his readers to trust in their faithful God, the One sovereign even over their trials. According to James, God uses trials to develop believers' endurance so that together they would be characterized by completeness, wholeness (1:4).

These are also the very characteristics that describe orphan-minded churches. "There is an authenticity and honesty in these ministries," Paul told me. "Not much remains hidden because traumatized kids bring the church's true character to the surface and everything gets exposed. To the Lord, it's a beautiful thing."

How might James's audience progress in a distinctly Christian quality of life? James wrote that they should ask God for wisdom in their trials and respond by humbly receiving His word of instruction.[5] As a dispersed people, these believers had been removed from their vocations and spheres of commerce, which resulted in them struggling in poverty. And much of James's argument for his audience to be mature in the faith rested on their need to trust God alone to supply their daily essentials. Thus, if a rich person and a poor one entered their corporate gathering, the latter should receive equal treatment as the former—since God and not the rich could provide the congregation's necessities.[6] Likewise, in entrepreneurial endeavors, the audience should recognize God's providence and resist the impure, selfish tendency that attempts to amass wealth independent of God.[7] Why was James so concerned for his audience to resist reliance on a wealthy benefactor or potentially lucrative business venture? Because the trials of dispersion and poverty placed his audience in a position to work out their faith, in part, by relying upon God to meet their needs.[8]

## How Does James 1:27 Fit In?

The religious, social, and economic grid of James's audience placed orphans and widows at a point of peril.[9] If the church did not come to their aid, no one would. But to James, the vulnerable situation of orphans and widows was actually a provision for the congregation. The needy—like kids in foster care and orphanages—give the church an at-hand, shovel-ready opportunity to practice our religion.[10] Throughout his epistle, James argued that by practicing their religion of trust in God and unflinching devotion to Him, the church would become mature, whole, complete. And James used two further adjectives in describing the religion he wished for the audience to carry out in relation to the needy among them: "Pure and undefiled religion in the sight of our God and Father is this: to visit orphans and widows in their distress, and to keep oneself unstained by the world" (James 1:27). Author Peter Davids noted that the combination of the adjectives *pure* and *undefiled* has a rhetorical punch, emphasizing both the presence of a positive element and the absence of a negative one. In other words, "absolute purity" was James's idea.[11]

The idea of "visit" in James 1:27 ranges with the distance separating the visitor and the visited. It could imply that the subject of the verb—the visitor—would leave a location and travel to another location with a view to assisting someone at the point of destination and then returning to their original location. More generally, as with orphans or widows who may not have had a stable location where they might receive a visitor, "looking after" one in need refers to being proximal to them day-by-day. That is, the idea of "visit" may require the subject to personally care for them on an ongoing basis, living in the same quarters, if you will. In *Counter Culture*,

> *The idea calls for the church to rearrange its time and resources, even to the degree of sacrifice, for the sake of the vulnerable.*

David Platt explained, "When the Bible describes 'visiting' orphans and widows here, it means more than simply saying hello to them every once in a while. . . . to visit orphans and widows means to seek them out with a deep concern for their well-being and a clear commitment to care for their needs."[12] To James, the idea calls for the church to rearrange its time and resources, even to the degree of sacrifice, for the sake of the vulnerable.

But James was not concerned only for the needs of the needy. He saw in the congregation a need for maturity that could be met as the church gave itself to those from whom they could receive no worldly benefit. By looking after orphans and widows, he wrote in the last part of James 1:27, the church fulfills the kinds of tasks necessary to keep itself unstained by the world. The religious situation of the congregation may have led to such severe persecution that children were orphaned the moment their parents were martyred. The economic conditions the congregation had to endure may have led to family poverty and dispersion of children. James's concern was for the orphan (that their needs would be met) and for his audience (that they practice their faith with purity). According to James, for the church to ignore or abdicate the needs of orphans was akin to hypocrisy—the very opposite of his exhortation for the audience to be mature and complete, perfected in their trial. David Platt continued James's line of thinking by challenging the modern-day church:

> We are a people happy to go to church just so long as nothing in our lives has to change. We are a people glad to be Christians just so long as we can define Christianity according to what accommodates us. The only problem is that in order for the religion of Christianity to be authentic, true, and actually

acceptable before God, we have to let Him define what it looks like.[13]

## The Effect of Example

When Paul Chitwood was the executive director of the Kentucky Baptist Convention, he witnessed many instances of how leaders set the example for their congregations. One in particular sticks in his mind. "We were helping a church plant. That pastor had three biological children and adopted two special needs kids. He has just now adopted an infant. He led by example and now the church is full of foster/adoptive parents." Indeed, the combination of skilled family leadership and hospitality noted as qualifications for pastoral leadership in 1 Timothy 3:1–7 and Titus 1:5–9[14] would supply what orphans need. Orphan care is not easy. Given the trauma that children have experienced long before they've entered our homes and churches, it's understandable that they generally have behavioral issues that can challenge parents and any siblings in the home and in church. This is why we need one another. This is the power of the church at its best. To lead by example.

"Good leadership is not determined in the absence of difficulty," wrote Bryan Chapell, "but in the prudent discipline and handling of problems when difficulties come."[15] Who in the church would be better qualified than elders to handle the behaviors orphans might exhibit? What is more, as a leader in the local church congregation, the pastor would naturally be able to connect family-less children with the family of God, a true forever family.

I recognize that pastors and their families feel maxed-out by the routines of ministry—establishing their vision in the church, helping the congregation take the gospel to the world, fighting cultural sins like racism, abortion, and sexual perversion. But herein lies the irony. As pastors welcome orphans into their homes, they progress in these very tasks. Pastoral orphan care demonstrates exemplary leadership, takes the gospel to the lost, counters the argument for abortion rights, reduces the possibility that orphans might become victims of sex-trafficking, and frequently demonstrates how the gospel breaks racial divisions. We have no excuse. As R. Kent Hughes pointed out, "Worship that pleases God involves throwing ourselves on the altar and before the needy world in service. We may plead a lack of time, but if we have time for recreation and social visits we have the time!"[16] And time devoted to orphan-care ministries is time invested in the congregation. As the church sees the pastor enduring in love to kids with physical, behavioral, or emotional challenges, believers receive a pattern for practicing their faith (Heb. 13:7). They know they have church leaders who can sympathize with them when the going gets tough. The leader's example can actually multiply the effect the church might have on both orphans and the culture.

I deeply understand the role the church must play. I am the result of a teen pregnancy that predates *Roe v. Wade* by just over one year. God placed me in a loving family and church where I was influenced by the gospel. God gave me a wife who is concerned for the gospel, the church, and the needs of vulnerable kids. God called me to lead a church that is concerned for practicing its faith by heeding His Word and caring for His reputation in the world. I'm living proof that God's reputation through the church is magnified as we partner together—leaders and congregation—to do good works that reflect God's love for us. As we work together to welcome children into our families, we display God. What an amazing opportunity the church— you!—have to shine in the darkness. And you can start today.

## DISCUSSION AND REFLECTION

- Why do you think the woman in Rio wanted Paul and Michelle Chitwood to take her daughter with them when they returned to the States? How did that experience impact the Chitwoods? How do you think you would have felt if you were in their place? Why?

- In what ways does your church organize wrap-around ministries for those who take children into their homes? How might you participate in wrap-around care?

- What is the context of James 1:27? How does caring for orphans and widows meet the needs of the church?

- Besides orphan care, how else might your church need to work out its faith?

- In what ways might you partner with the pastoral leadership in your church to create a culture of foster care and adoption?

- What do you sense God leading *you* to do to bring children into the homes of your church?

# Appendix

---

# Five Essential Relationships to Cultivate as You Foster or Adopt[1]

As I interviewed the people in this book, as well as what I've learned in my own adoption experience with my daughters, I've thought a lot about what it takes to be "successful" in foster-care and adoption ministries. It comes down to relationships. Five parenting ministry partnerships, in particular, that can anchor you as you foster or adopt.

## Relationship #1: Your Spouse

As you foster or adopt, the first relationship to cultivate is with your spouse. Foster care or adoption will stretch your marriage in ways it has never been stretched before. In the comedy (or was it a *documentary?*) *Instant Family*, characters played by Mark Wahlberg and Rose Byrne attend their first post-placement

foster-parent meeting and share that everything is wonderful in
their home, their marriage is fulfilled as never before. By the next
meeting, Wahlburg and Byrne are at each other's throats, and
Byrne is needing shots of liquor to make it through the day. Kids
coming into your home will bring you and your spouse to wits'
end too. Because you both will be emotionally drained, you will
be vulnerable to selfishness and the blame game.

These four steps will help you develop a parenting ministry partnership with each other and will help you stay strong
together.

### Spend Time with Kids the Age(s) You Hope to Foster or Adopt

While no two kids are the same, if you and your spouse can
together get a framework for how kids generally think and act,
you will be better equipped for those who will come into your
home. Babysit friends' kids. Work in the church nursery. Organize a childcare night for your church. Volunteer on consecutive
days at a children's shelter or at a local school.

### Read Books on Parenting and Theology

The resources I've mentioned in this book offer principles
that you and your spouse must discuss and come to terms with
if you are going to stay married as foster or adoptive parents. And
read theology so you are not just thinking about yourselves and
your kids. Books like J. I. Packer's *Knowing God* will buoy you
for the lonely, reverent road ahead.

### Try New, Challenging Experiences Together

Do an escape room. Eat Chinese food with chopsticks, using
your less dominant hand. Run a 10K. Volunteer to clean the

toilets at a local truck stop. Find your physical and emotional service limits and push through them. Kids will push you more, so get ready.

### Enjoy Frequent Marital Intimacy

When things get tough with kids, marital intimacy will become a spiritual discipline. You will need that time together to maintain an emotional connection. The bedroom will become a place of private worship and recreation, a place just for the two of you to be vulnerable and unashamed before God.

## Relationship #2: Your Local Church

The New Testament describes believers as parts of the same body, members of one another (see Rom. 12:3–8; 1 Cor. 12:4–31; Eph. 4:1–16, 25). If you have not already committed to a local church, then I encourage you to do so. This will allow your church leaders and your brothers and sisters in Christ there to know that you wish to partner with them in gospel ministry— and wish for them to partner with you in the ministry of foster care or adoption.

Did you notice I use the same language to describe your relationship with your spouse and your local church? Partnership. As a member of the body of Christ in a local church, you enjoy a mutual commitment with other believers that reflects your relationship with your spouse. To help your local church partner well with you in your foster or adoption journey, I suggest you connect with the following:

### A Pastor

I am not concerned here with the leadership structure of your church, just get in touch with the pastor you know best at your church and let them know of your burden to foster or adopt. Whether your church has a membership of fifty, five hundred, or five thousand, informing the pastoral leadership of your plans will be step one in helping the church join with you in your parenting ministry. So make an appointment and share your heart. Don't think that the pastoral staff is too busy—God's work in your life is what they live for! And don't be offended if they ask hard questions about your preparedness—that is why God has them in your life.

### A Small Group Leader

Whether your church has Sunday school classes, adult Bible fellowship or home groups, connect with whomever you are closest to. Speak to them privately about your plans to foster or adopt before announcing your plans publicly to the group. This will ensure the leader is on your team and will allow that person an opportunity to arrange the best time for you to share your news with the group at a gathered meeting. Your small group will play a vital role in the success of your foster or adoption ministry. Along the way, they will support you with prayer, meals, visitation, babysitting, and verbal encouragement.

### Nursery, Children's Ministry, and Youth Leaders

The nursery, children's, and youth staff need to know the details of your ministry and they need to know your kids personally. It may be that the children who come into your home will have never attended a church gathering. When the kids get into nursery, Sunday school, or youth group, there is little chance they will not struggle. By connecting these church leaders with your kids personally, outside of church gatherings, you will provide a framework for relational discipleship. The more comfortable your kids are with those who lead the children's and youth ministries of your church, the more comfortable your church will be in partnering with you for parenting ministry over the long haul.

## Relationship #3: The Children You Already Have

Parents who enter foster-care or adoption ministry with biological children already in the home will face specific challenges. To the degree that those children are able, they should be involved in the process of welcoming new siblings. Here are three principles for developing a parenting ministry partnership with children already in the home.

### See Foster or Adoption Ministry as Discipleship—Yours and Theirs

Parents who are discipling the children already in their home will notice that sharing a desire to foster or adopt will not seem strange. As parents lead their children to read Scripture, participate in the life of their local congregation, pray for missionaries, and stay informed about the needs of their communities, the topic of orphan care will surface regularly.

### Date the Kids You Have—and Continue to Do So

Your kids need to know that you will be there for them when the new kids arrive, and next year too. Before the new kids arrive, mark the calendar with specific activities you will do with kids already in the home, one-on-one dates or trips to their favorite stores or events. Be sure to fulfill that commitment. In doing so, you will show your current kids that you are devoted to them. Help them see that they are not losing you as a parent. Give them a vision for expansion, not contraction. As they see you expanding your parenting to include the new kids in your home while devoting yourself to them, they will be ready to expand their capacity to be a brother or sister to the new kids God has given you.

### Evaluate with Your Kids Along the Way

Partnerships rise and fall on the fulcrum of communication. So partner with the kids in your home by including them in the evaluation process of how the foster or adoption ministry is going. Inquire about their perspective, how they feel about the process and about the new kids sharing their living space. Be honest in your evaluation of the good, bad, and ugly. Your honesty will help them be transparent about their perspective.

## Relationship #4: Your Parents

If couples who plan to foster or adopt can enlist the support of their own parents, they will have a greater degree of connectivity with the kids coming into their home. Grandparents provide foster or adopted kids a sense of belonging in their new family.

The degree of commitment grandparents may wish to offer in this partnership may be high or low. Whatever the circumstances, potential foster or adoptive couples should court their parents and patiently give them a vision for multigenerational influence. Beware: your parents will likely try to talk you out of it! They have probably heard horror stories, and they want to prevent harm in your home. Don't expect balloons and streamers when you approach Mom and Dad—but approach them anyway. Their involvement, even in small ways, can help your kids feel connected to you—and that is what you need. So be confident as you inform your parents about the ministry God has called you to fulfill. Trust me here: most grandparents warm up to foster or adopted kids over time. Your parents' first reaction will likely be their worst reaction. Be prepared and get it out of the way.

Some grandparents hesitate to support their children's desire to foster or adopt because they know their family might become multiracial. As I note in part 5, compared with the population at large, there are a disproportionate number of minority—especially African American—children in foster care. Thus, it may be the case that God would use your minority-race kids to help your parents see the racial bias in their own lives. Let me offer three specific ideas for developing a multigenerational parenting partnership with your parents.

### *Share with Them Early in the Process*

If you are talking with friends at church about your plans to enroll in foster-care class, you would do well to talk with your parents too. Even if you feel your parents will not be supportive, make an appointment to speak with them. The last thing you want is for your parents to find out secondhand that you are planning to bring foster kids into your home. Yikes! Try to have a formal, sit-down meal or meeting with your parents and share your heart. Allow them to ask questions. Don't get defensive. Don't feel you have to have all the answers. Be confident. Be calm, patient, even teachable.

*Involve Your Parents in the Process and at Special Events*

Grandparents will begin to warm up to God's call on your life as they become informed on the process. Once they see profiles of neglected and abused kids, most grandparents see why their kids are responding to God's call. So keep your parents in the loop on classes, certifications, and specific kids who are available to be fostered or adopted. Talk with your parents about their expectations. It might be good to give them a copy of this book. Introduce the kids to your parents at the earliest convenient opportunity. On move-in day, have parents participate in whatever ways they feel comfortable. Let your parents know of birthdays and activities, and ask your parents how they might want to participate.

*Facilitate Opportunities for Your Parents to Disciple Your Foster or Adopted Kids*

If your parents are believers and supportive, encourage them to pray for your kids and look for opportunities to engage them in spiritual matters. If possible, have a time of Scripture reading and prayer when your parents are visiting. For Christian grandparents, few opportunities bring more joy than evangelizing and discipling their grandkids.

## Relationship #5: Local Schools They Might Attend

You will be more likely to connect with your new kids when they arrive if you have already connected with the school they might attend. Though homeschooling or private schooling might be an option for educating foster kids, courts and agencies will nearly always require parents to place kids in public school. School, not the same school necessarily (because foster kids often move from one school to another when they have a change of placement) but school as an institution, is home. School provides stable relationships and routines, food, emotional boundaries, friends, and activities. School is life for foster kids, so develop a partnership with the local school your child will attend. This will help you as a parent connect with your kids. I suggest at least two steps.

### *Visit the School Before the Child Is Placed in Your Home*

Make an appointment to meet the principal, guidance counselor, homeroom teacher, and nurse. Share with them as much information as possible. Don't think you are imposing. You will make their jobs easier if you prepare them to welcome your child's arrival. This is a crucial step in your foster or adoption ministry—even if you give the school just a few days' notice of the child's arrival. If you know that your child has a special medication schedule (most foster kids are prescribed behavior-regulation meds), let the school know. If your child has an interest in an extracurricular activity or sport, connect with the coaches or staff.

### *Volunteer at the School Routinely, Even Before the Child Is Placed in Your Home*

If you want the school to partner with you, partner with them. If you connect with the school your child will attend, your child will know you are committed to them as an individual. Make that school your primary focus of community ministry, and you will help your child connect with you. I suggest volunteering for a short period of time, perhaps an hour or two, multiple times per week. This will help you get to know routines and people—those whom you may want to keep away from your child and those whom you want to connect with your child. Heed the advice of the school administration on what volunteer opportunities might help you connect with the school and help your child to connect as well. After the child is placed in your home, continue volunteering on the same schedule. If your partnership is a win for the school, it will likely be a win for you and your child.

# Acknowledgments

First, I wish to express thanks to Drew Dyck, Randall Payleitner, Ginger Kolbaba, and the team at Moody Publishers. Their creativity and support gave me joy in writing each chapter. At the conclusion of a project, an author will often state that their work is better because of the editorial team they worked with along the way. I concur here.

This book was a collaborative project. Many of the eighteen individuals or couples I profiled gave of their time so I could interview them. Doug Webster, Russell Moore, Tate Williams, Tony Merida, Jason Johnson, Bishop Aaron Blake, Bob Miller, John Mark Yeats, John Moore, D. J. Jordan, Heidi Olson, Rhi, Karen Countryman-Roswurm, Jeff Dodge, Kevin and Lynette Ezell (while they were on vacation!), and Paul Chitwood. I am thankful for their generous contribution, but even more for their faithfulness to God's call on their lives.

Dr. Jason Allen, president of Midwestern Baptist Theological Seminary (MBTS), has cultivated a partnership with Moody Publishers, and I am grateful for his visionary leadership at For the Church. Dr. Jason Duesing, provost at MBTS, also helped to connect my vision with Moody. Kevin Choi, my research fellow, proofread the manuscript and offered helpful suggestions along the way.

I personally know of an orphan-minded church—The Master's Community Church in Kansas City, Kansas, where I pastor. Besides all that I noted in Part 1, I am grateful for the prayer support they have provided during this book project. The intercession and support of church members Jim and Diane Langdon, in whose vacation home my family and I stayed while touring Charleston, South Carolina, is worth special mention. On at least two specific occasions when I was praying with men of our church regarding the book, I received email notifications from Drew Dyck at Moody Publishers regarding their interest in my ideas. Thanks, Ryan Thompson and Skye Singleton.

I am especially grateful to my wife, Julie, for her partnership and vision for the gospel, the church, and the needs of orphans. Her enthusiasm has established an environment for our biological kids, J. T., Anna, Sarah, Grace, and Chesed, to open their arms to our adopted daughters. Finally, I wish to thank my mother, Phyllis Chipman, and Julie's parents, Lee and Susan Moore, for welcoming our adopted girls into their hearts, just as they have all their other grandkids.

# Notes

### Chapter 1: Born on the Right Side of History—Barely

1. For counsel and encouragement on childlessness, see Chelsea Patterson Sobolik, *Longing for Motherhood: Holding on to Hope in the Midst of Childlessness* (Chicago: Moody, 2018).

### Chapter 2: "We Want to Adopt You!"

1. Not their real names.
2. Russell Moore, *Adopted for Life: The Priority of Adoption for Christian Families and Churches,* updated and expanded edition (Wheaton, IL: Crossway, 2015).
3. "Your wife shall be like a fruitful vine within your house, your children like olive plants around your table."

### Chapter 4: How Many First-Born Children Can a Couple Have?

1. *The Spirit of Adoption: Writers on Religion, Adoption, Faith, and More*, Melanie Springer Mock, Martha Kalnin Diede, and Jeremiah Webster, eds. (Eugene, OR: Cascade, 2014). Doug wrote a chapter in the book as well, reflecting on the frantic week in 1979 when he and Virginia got the call from the social worker that they could pick up Jeremiah the next day.
2. David Platt, *Counter Culture: Following Christ in an Anti-Christian Age* (Carol Stream, IL: Tyndale, 2015), 81.
3. David Prince, "What Are We For?" in *The Gospel and Adoption*, ed. Russell Moore and Andrew T. Walker (Nashville: B&H Publishing Group, 2017), 23.

### Chapter 5: What Does Spiritual Warfare Have to Do with Orphan Care?

1. Russell Moore, *Adopted for Life: The Priority of Adoption for Christian Families and Churches,* updated and expanded edition (Wheaton, IL: Crossway, 2015), 17.
2. The ERLC is an entity of the Southern Baptist Convention, engaging the culture with the gospel of Jesus Christ. For more information, see https://erlc.com/about.
3. Moore, *Adopted for Life,* 227.
4. Ibid., 230.
5. Ibid., 174.
6. Ibid., 233.

### Chapter 6: Taking a Jet Plane into the Earthquake Zone

1. See Luke 6:30, 34, 36.
2. Craig L. Blomberg, *Jesus and the Gospels: An Introduction and Survey,* 2nd ed. (Nashville: B&H Academic, 2009), 170.
3. Ruth Anne Burrell, "Steps of Faith: Tate Williams," The Global Orphan Project," January 26, 2015, http://www.ruthanneburrell.com/blog/2015/01/26/steps-of-faith-tate-williams-the-global-orphan-project/.
4. Scot McKnight, *Sermon on the Mount,* vol. 21, *The Story of God Bible Commentary* series (Grand Rapids, MI: Zondervan, 2013), 219.

### Chapter 7: How Many Continents Can You Get into One House?

1. David Platt, *Counter Culture: Following Christ in an Anti-Christian Age* (Carol Stream, IL: Tyndale, 2015), 80.
2. Ibid., 81.
3. Collin Hansen, "Platt Commissioned by Brook Hills in Final Sunday as Senior Pastor," The Gospel Coalition, September 15, 2014, https://www.thegospelcoalition.org/article/platt-commissioned-by-brook-hills-in-final-sunday-as-senior-pastor.
4. Heather Platt, "God's Sovereignty and Orphan Care: One Mom's Encouragement," Radical, January 24, 2017, http://radical.net/articles/gods-sovereignty-and-orphan-care-one-moms-encouragement/.
5. Platt, *Counter Culture,* 91–92.
6. Ibid., 97.
7. Ibid., 98.

### Chapter 8: Counterfeit Hospitality Not Welcome Here

1. Rosaria Butterfield, *The Secret Thoughts of an Unlikely Convert* (Pittsburgh: Crown & Covenant, 2012), 11.
2. Ibid., 33.
3. Rosaria Butterfield, *The Gospel Comes with a House Key: Practicing Radically Ordinary Hospitality in Our Post-Christian World* (Wheaton, IL: Crossway, 2018), 21.
4. Ibid., 24.
5. Ibid., 215.
6. Darrell L. Bock, *Luke 9:51–24:53,* in *Baker Exegetical Commentary on the New Testament* series (Grand Rapids, MI: Baker, 1996), 1257.
7. Butterfield, *Secret Thoughts,* 119.
8. Ibid.
9. Ibid.
10. Butterfield, *The Gospel Comes with a Housekey,* 116.
11. Butterfield, *Secret Thoughts,* 124.

### Chapter 9: Bedrooms, Birthday Parties, and the Gospel

1. Tony's observation is similar to Russell Moore's statement: "What better way is there to bring the good news of Christ than to see his unwanted little brothers and sisters placed in families where they'll be raised in the

nurture and admonition of the Lord?" (Russell Moore, *Adopted for Life: The Priority of Adoption for Christian Families and Churches,* updated and expanded edition [Wheaton, IL: Crossway, 2015], 68).

2. Imago Dei is the home of 127Worldwide (www.127worldwide.org). Named after James 1:27, 127Worldwide facilitates short-term mission trips to regions where poverty has placed children and widows in dire circumstances. Often, orphanages in countries like Kenya, Uganda, and Guatemala are their destinations. Imago Dei also partners with Lifesong for Orphans (www.lifesong.org), a ministry that works to help each believer serve the orphan, "some to adopt, some to care, some to give."

3. Craig L. Blomberg, *Neither Poverty nor Riches: A Biblical Theology of Possessions* (Downers Grove, IL: IVP, 1999), 178.

4. Douglas J. Moo, *Romans,* in *The NIV Application Commentary* series (Grand Rapids, MI: Zondervan, 2000), 489.

5. Tony Merida and Rick Morton, *Orphanology: Awakening to Gospel-Centered Adoption and Orphan Care* (Birmingham, AL: New Hope, 2011), 81–83.

**Chapter 10: Flip the Script**

1. Jason Johnson, *Reframing Foster Care: Filtering Your Foster Parenting Journey through the Lens of the Gospel* (Grand Rapids, MI: Credo House, 2018), 151.

2. Ibid., 139.

3. Gordon D. Fee, *The First Epistle to the Corinthians,* in *New International Commentary on the New Testament* series (Grand Rapids, MI: Eerdmans, 1987), 625.

4. Rosaria Butterfield, *The Gospel Comes with a House Key: Practicing Radically Ordinary Hospitality in Our Post-Christian World* (Wheaton, IL: Crossway, 2018), 216.

5. D. A. Carson, *The Cross and Christian Ministry: Leadership Lessons from 1 Corinthians* (Grand Rapids, MI: Baker, 1993), 97.

**Chapter 11: Trial by Fire**

1. Jason Weber, "One Question from a Pastor Changed Things for Hundreds in Foster Care," Christian Alliance for Orphans, August 5, 2016, https://cafo.org/2016/08/05/one-question-pastor-changed-things-hundreds-foster-care/.

2. "United States: Quick Facts," United States Census Bureau, accessed March 3, 2019, https://www.census.gov/quickfacts/fact/table/US/PST045217, and "Foster Care Statistics 2016," Childwelfare.gov, accessed March 3, 2019, https://www.childwelfare.gov/pubPDFs/foster.pdf#page=8&view=Race%20and%20ethnicity.

3. "Stand Sunday: The Story of a Movement," CarePortal, accessed February 28, 2019, https://careportal.org/resources/stand-sunday-video/.

4. Jason Weber, "One Question from a Pastor Changed Things for Hundreds in Foster Care," Christian Alliance for Orphans, August 5,

2016, https://cafo.org/2016/08/05/one-question-pastor-changed-things-hundreds-foster-care/.

5. "Care Portal," accessed February 28, 2019, https://careportal.org/.
6. "Engrafted: When the Kids Burn Down the House," Christian Alliance for Orphans, accessed February 28, 2019, video 5:25, https://vimeo.com/236147986.
7. Diego Fuller, "Engrafted Intro (feat. Morsello)," May 27, 2014.

## Chapter 12: Might a Social Worker Be Your Next Church Hire?

1. R. Kent Hughes, *Hebrews: An Anchor for the Soul,* vol. 2; *Preach the Word* series (Wheaton, IL: Crossway, 1993), 37.
2. F. F. Bruce, *Hebrews,* rev. ed., *New International Commentary on the New Testament* series Grand Rapids, MI: Eerdmans, 1990), 101.
3. Russell Moore, *Adopted for Life: The Priority of Adoption for Christian Families and Churches,* updated and expanded edition (Wheaton, IL: Crossway, 2015), 173.
4. Mez McConnell and Mike McKinley, *Church in Hard Places: How the Local Church Brings Life to the Poor and Needy* (Wheaton, IL: Crossway, 2016), 174.

## Chapter 13: No Race Left Out

1. Douglas J. Moo, *Romans,* in *The NIV Application Commentary* series (Grand Rapids, MI: Zondervan, 2000), 51.
2. J. Daniel Hays, *From Every People and Nation,* vol. 14 in *New Studies in Biblical Theology* series (Downers Grove, IL: IVP, 2003), 200.
3. Jarvis J. Williams, *One New Man: The Cross and Racial Reconciliation in Pauline Theology* (Nashville: B&H Academic, 2010), 57.

## Chapter 14: Transracial Adoption Comes to Television

1. In 2018, a US District Court judge struck down the Indian Child Welfare Act of 1978, concluding that it unconstitutionally provides Native American families preferential treatment in adoptions of Native American children, violating the Fifth Amendment's guarantee of equal protection. Meagan Flynn, "Court Strikes Down Native American Adoption Law, Saying It Discriminates Against Non-Native Americans," *Washington Post,* October 10, 2018, https://www.washingtonpost.com/news/morning-mix/wp/2018/10/10/court-strikes-down-native-american-adoption-law-saying-it-discriminates-against-non-native-americans/?utm_term=.e30d7953a9dd. John Moore responds to that decision in his article, "On Indian Child Welfare Act, Time for Critics and Supporters to Talk in Earnest," *The Chronicle of Social Change,* October 17, 2018, https://chronicleofsocialchange.org/icwa/indian-child-welfare-act-time-for-critics-supporters-talk-earnest/32509.
2. "Adoption Controversy: Battle Over Baby Veronica," *Dr. Phil,* posted June 6, 2013, CBS Television, https://www.drphil.com/shows/1895/.

3. G. K. Beale, *The Temple and the Church's Mission: A Biblical Theology of the Dwelling Place of God,* vol 17 in *New Studies in Biblical Theology* series (Downers Grove, IL: IVP, 2004), 262–63.

4. Russell Moore, *Adopted for Life: The Priority of Adoption for Christian Families and Churches,* updated and expanded edition (Wheaton, IL: Crossway, 2015), 34–35.

5. Jarvis J. Williams, *One New Man: The Cross and Racial Reconciliation in Pauline Theology* (Nashville: B&H Academic, 2010), 135.

6. Focus on the Family, "Wait No More," accessed March 1, 2019, https://www.focusonthefamily.com/about/ministry-programs.

7. Christian Alliance for Orphans, "CAFO Summit," accessed March 1, 2019, https://cafo.org/summit/.

**Chapter 15: Racial Profiling and Forgiveness of Sin**

1. "United States: Quick Facts," United States Census Bureau, accessed March 3, 2019, https://www.census.gov/quickfacts/fact/table/US/PST045217, and "Foster Care Statistics 2016," Childwelfare.gov, accessed March 3, 2019, https://www.childwelfare.gov/pubPDFs/foster.pdf#page=8&view=Race%20and%20ethnicit.

2. Tony Merida and Rick Morton, *Orphanology: Awakening to Gospel-Centered Adoption and Orphan Care,* (Birmingham, AL: New Hope, 2011), 84.

3. David Francis, "Poverty and Mistreatment of Children go Hand in Hand," The National Bureau of Economic Research, accessed May 15, 2019, https://www.nber.org/digest/jan00/w7343.html; "Neighborhoods," Child Welfare Information Gateway, U.S. Department of Health & Human Services, accessed May 15, 2019, https://www.childwelfare.gov/topics/can/factors/environmental/neighborhoods/.

4. "Raising Black Children in a Multiracial Family," CAFO Summit, held Thursday, May 10, 2018, at Stonebriar Community Church, Frisco, TX, https://cafo.org/summit/workshops/.

**Chapter 16: Why the Local Pimp Does Not Want You to Foster or Adopt**

1. "Safety, Care & Nurturing Clinic," Children's Mercy, accessed March 3, 2019, https://www.childrensmercy.org/departments-and-clinics/child-adversity-and-resilience/safety-care-and-nurturing/.

2. "Sex-trafficking," Centers for Disease Control and Prevention," accessed March 3, 2019, https://www.cdc.gov/violenceprevention/sexualviolence/trafficking.html.

3. Heidi Olson, "Recognizing Human Trafficking for Health Care Workers," The Children's Mercy Hospital, accessed March 3, 2019, https://www.cmics.org/pbp/LoadImagesFiles/LoadFile?contentGUID=5EB6F7E4-BEED-4D18-8E81-8AC4143CD533.

4. Jennifer Hansen, MD, "Child Sex-trafficking in our Communities," The Children's Mercy Hospital, accessed March 3, 2019, https://www.childrensmercy.org/siteassets/media-documents-for-depts-section/

documents-for-health-care-providers/nursing-childsex-trafficking.pdf.
5. "Traffickers will often send one of their girls into group homes to find girls and urge them to leave by saying things like they will be well taken care of financially and have a 'family' so to speak who will care for them" (Dawn Post, "Why Human Traffickers Prey on Foster Kids," CityLimits.org, January 23, 2015, https://citylimits.org/2015/01/23/why-traffickers-prey-on-foster-care-kids).
6. Holly V. Hays, "Ahead of Indy 500, Residents Urged to Look for Signs of Human Trafficking," Indystar.com, updated May 24, 2018, https://www.indystar.com/story/news/crime/2018/05/24/indy-500-impd-human-trafficking-ahead-race/634131002/.
7. Darrell L. Bock, *Jesus According to Scripture: Restoring the Portrait from the Gospels* (Grand Rapids, MI: Baker, 2002), 255.
8. Sarah Plake, "Children abusing children: Children's Mercy sees dangerous trend involving children and porn," 41 Action News KSHB.com, November 30, 2018, https://www.kshb.com/news/local-news/children-abusing-children-childrens-mercy-sees-dangerous-trend-involving-children-and-porn.

**Chapter 17: The Pimp's Chief Operating Officer: A Woman**

1. "Child Sexual Exploitation Ring: Collaborative Law Enforcement Efforts Dismantle Conspiracy," FBI News, February 27, 2018, https://www.fbi.gov/news/stories/ohio-child-sex-trafficking-ring-dismantled.
2. Ellen Wulfhorst, "Without Family, U.S. Children in Foster Care Easy Prey for Human Traffickers," Rueters, May 3, 2018, https://www.reuters.com/article/us-usa-trafficking-fostercare/without-family-u-s-children-in-foster-care-easy-prey-for-human-traffickers-idUSKBN1I-40OM.
3. Matthew Johnson and Merideth Dank, Ph.D., "The Hustle: Economics of the Underground Commercial Sex Industry," Urban Institute, accessed March 3, 2019, http://apps.urban.org/features/theHustle/index.html.
4. Gary M. Burge, *John,* in *The NIV Application Commentary* series (Grand Rapids, MI: Zondervan, 2000), 142.

**Chapter 18: The Family of God as the Place to Belong**

1. Karen I. Countryman-Roswurm, *Girls Like You, Girls Like Me: An Analysis of Domestic Minor Sex-trafficking and the Development of a Risk and Resiliency Assessment For Sexually Exploited Youth,* Ph.D. dissertation, May, 2012, xxxiii, https://studylib.net/doc/14330331/girls-like-you--girls-like-me--and-the-development-of. "Training Aims to Help Local Faith Leaders to Fight Human Trafficking," *The Sunflower,* January 12, 2015, https://thesunflower.com/5264/news/training-aims-to-help-local-faith-leaders-to-fight-human-trafficking/.
2. "Street Outreach Services (SOS)," Wichita Children's Home, accessed March 2, 2019, https://wch.org/services/street-outreach.

3. L. Whitbeck, D. Hoyt, and A. M. Cauce, *The Midwest Longitudinal Study of Homeless Adolescents*, National Clearinghouse on Homeless Youth and Families, accessed March 2, 2019, https://rhyclearinghouse .acf.hhs.gov/library/2001/midwest-longitudinal-study-homeless-adolescents.

4. "Policy Development," Center for Combatting Human Trafficking, accessed March 2, 2019, http://combatinghumantrafficking.org/Services/ Policy_Development.aspx.

5. "Office of Juvenile Justice Detention Prevention," U.S. Department of Justice, accessed March 2, 2019, https://www.ojjdp.gov/.

6. "Direct Service," Center for Combatting Human Trafficking, accessed March 2, 2019, http://combatinghumantrafficking.org/Services/Direct_ Service.aspx.

7. Michael Dolce, "We Have Set Up a System to Sex-Traffic American Children," *Newsweek*, January 12, 2018, https://www.newsweek.com/ we-have-set-system-sex-traffic-american-children-779541.

8. Katherine Burgess, "Runaway Foster Kids Raise Sex-Trafficking Fears in Kansas," *The Wichita Eagle*, updated February 19, 2018, https://www .kansas.com/news/local/article200579429.html.

## Chapter 19: Leading from the Front

1. In the pastoral epistles, the roles Timothy and Titus took up were distinct from the pastoral offices they were laboring to establish. Though Timothy and Titus did not function as shepherds of the local church in Ephesus or on the island of Crete, they were nonetheless to exemplify the characteristics Paul wished for pastors to exhibit in pastoral work. For distinctions between the ministries of Timothy and Titus and local pastors that would come after them, see Benjamin L. Merkle, "Ecclesiology in the Pastoral Epistles," in *Entrusted with the Gospel* (Nashville: Broadman & Holman, 2010), 194–98.

2. Thorvald B. Madsen III noted the coherent frame of beliefs and behavior in the pastoral epistles: "The Pastoral Epistles contain two types of statements related to proper conduct. Some of them capture various aspects of the Christian worldview, declaring what God is like and what he has done for particular groups of people—Paul, Timothy, the church, and so forth. Others state or imply what the affected person's duties are, given that same set of facts. In this sense, the Pastoral Epistles dwell on the *basis* for Christian conduct, as opposed to merely drawing boundaries for action." Thorvald B. Madsen III, "The Ethics of the Pastoral Epistles," in *Entrusted with the Gospel* (Nashville: Broadman & Holman, 2010), 219.

3. "Just as an architect might sketch a pattern before adding the details, or as an artist might sketch the design of a painting before completing it, or as a writer may start with an outline of a paper before writing the manuscript, so Timothy was to follow Paul's outline—and then expound and apply it. Timothy was not told to make up his own outline, add to

it, or take away from it. He was to take what Paul taught and teach it to others." Tony Merida, *Christ-Centered Exposition Commentary: Exalting Christ in 1 & 2 Timothy and Titus* (Nashville: B&H Publishing Group, 2013), 154.

4. "Vv. 6–8 take a somewhat different form because Paul is seeking to accomplish two or three things at once. He is urging younger men to live godly Christian lives, and he is addressing Titus about his particular responsibilities as a minister and as an example to these men" (George W. Knight III, *The Pastoral Epistles*, in *The New International Greek Testament Commentary* series [Grand Rapids, MI: Eerdmans, 1992], 311).

**Chapter 20: "If They Can Do It, Goodness, We Can Sure Do It!"**

1. Lynette Ezell, "You Can Do This: Here's Where You Begin," Send Relief, February 3, 2017, https://www.sendrelief.org/podcast-episode/you-can-do-this-heres-where-you-begin/.
2. Philip H. Towner, *1–2 Timothy & Titus*, in *The IVP New Testament Commentary* series (Downers Grove, IL: InterVarsity, 1994), 86.
3. David Platt, "1 Timothy," in *Christ-Centered Exposition Commentary: Exalting Jesus in 1 & 2 Timothy and Titus*, eds., David Platt, Daniel L. Akin, and Tony Merida (Nashville: B&H Publishing Group, 2013), 57.
4. David Prince, "What Are We For?" in *The Gospel and Adoption*, ed. Russell Moore and Andrew T. Walker (Nashville: B&H Publishing Group, 2017), 19.
5. I. Howard Marshall, *1 Peter*, in *The IVP New Testament Commentary* series (Downers Grove, IL: InterVarsity, 1991), 163–64.

**Chapter 21: Be the One?**

1. In 2018, Paul transitioned from leading the Kentucky Baptist Convention to acting as president of the International Mission Board (IMB) of the Southern Baptist Convention, expanding his influence for the gospel and needy kids around the world.
2. "Sunrise Children's Services," Accessed March 3, 2019, https://www.sunrise.org/our-history/.
3. See James 1:13–21; 3:7–12; 4:1–3, 11–12; 5:9.
4. See James 1:13–15; 2:1–7; 4:13–14.
5. See James 1:5–8, 16–25.
6. See James 2:1–13.
7. See James 4:13–17.
8. See James 2:14–26.
9. I recognize that James addresses the needs of both orphans and widows. Though widow care is not the specific concern of our topic, many principles set forth here could apply to how pastors might exemplify concern for widows as well.
10. "The matters James mentions in these verses were undoubtedly problems among the Christians to whom he is writing. But they are also frequently mentioned in Scripture as key components of a biblical

lifestyle. 'Looking after widows and orphans' picks up a frequent [Old Testament] refrain. In the ancient world, with an absence of money-making possibilities for women and any kind of social welfare, widows and orphans were helpless to provide for themselves. A mark of Israel's obedience, therefore, was to be a special concern for these helpless people" (Douglas J. Moo, *The Letter of James,* in *Pillar New Testament Commentary* series (Grand Rapids, MI: Eerdmans, 2000], 96–97).

11. Peter Davids, *The Epistle of James,* in *The New International Greek Testament Commentary* series [Grand Rapids, MI: Eerdmans, 1992), 102.

12. David Platt, *Counter Culture: Following Christ in an Anti-Christian Age* (Carol Stream, IL: Tyndale, 2015), 82.

13. David Platt, *Christ-Centered Exposition Commentary: Exalting Christ in James,* eds., David Platt, Daniel L. Akin, and Tony Merida (Nashville: B&H Publishing Group, 2014), 26.

14. Gordon D. Fee noted that in the ancient world it is probable that pastors of house churches were also the heads of the families in whose homes the churches met: "Thus . . . there is the closest kind of relationship between family and church" (Fee, *1 and 2 Timothy, Titus,* 82). The argument of this chapter extends the principle of Fee's observation and applies even to churches that gather outside of a pastor's residence. Who better to help the church meet the needs orphans—those who have no parents—than a pastor whose parenting skill is demonstrated in his home and before the church?

15. R. Kent Hughes and Bryan Chapell, *1 & 2 Timothy and Titus: To Guard the Deposit,* Preaching the Word Series (Wheaton, IL: Crossway, 2000), 297.

16. R. Kent Hughes, *James: Faith That Works,* Preaching the Word series (Wheaton, IL: Crossway, 1991), 84.

### Appendix: Five Essential Relationships to Cultivate as You Foster or Adopt

1. These ideas were first posted at ftc.co, https://ftc.co/resource-library/blog-entries/by-author/todd-chipman.

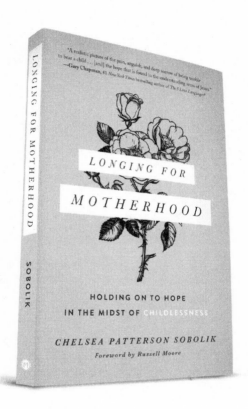